THE HUMID CONDITION

Before you start to read this book, take this moment to think about making a donation to punctum books, an independent non-profit press,

@ https://punctumbooks.com/support/

If you're reading the e-book, you can click on the image below to go directly to our donations site. Any amount, no matter the size, is appreciated and will help us to keep our ship of fools afloat. Contributions from dedicated readers will also help us to keep our commons open and to cultivate new work that can't find a welcoming port elsewhere. Our adventure is not possible without your support.

Vive la Open Access.

Fig. 1. Hieronymus Bosch, *Ship of Fools* (1490–1500)

THE HUMID CONDITION: (MORE) OVERHEATED OBSERVATIONS. Copyright © 2020 by Dominic Pettman. This work carries a Creative Commons BY-NC-SA 4.0 International license, which means that you are free to copy and redistribute the material in any medium or format, and you may also remix, transform and build upon the material, as long as you clearly attribute the work to the authors (but not in a way that suggests the authors or punctum books endorses you and your work), you do not use this work for commercial gain in any form whatsoever, and that for any remixing and transformation, you distribute your rebuild under the same license. http://creativecommons.org/licenses/by-nc-sa/4.0/

"Some Remarks on the Legacy of Madame Francine Descartes — First Lady and Historian of the Robocene — on the Occasion of 500 Years Since Her Unlawful Watery Execution" was first published online by the Public Domain Review in 2017. It is reprinted here with kind permission of PDR.

First published in 2020 by punctum books, Earth, Milky Way.
https://punctumbooks.com

ISBN-13: 978-1-950192-71-7 (print)
ISBN-13: 978-1-950192-72-4 (ePDF)

DOI: 10.21983/P3.0284.1.00

LCCN: 2020930972
Library of Congress Cataloging Data is available from the Library of Congress

Book design: Vincent W.J. van Gerven Oei

HIC SVNT MONSTRA

The Humid Condition
(More) Overheated Observations

Dominic Pettman

CONTENTS

The Humid Condition · 15

APPENDICES

Ersatz Haikus · 161

In Sweden · 171

The Thoughts · 175

Some Remarks on the Legacy of Madame Francine Descartes — First Lady and Historian of the Robocene — on the Occasion of 500 Years Since Her Unlawful Watery Execution · 179

…It's not the heat, it's the humanity.

Content Warning

The following pages contain all 26 alphabetical letters, in different combinations, arranged in a manner so as to hopefully convey meaning.

THE HUMID CONDITION

I have nothing (new) to say. And I'm saying it.

Please forgive the length of this manuscript, but I didn't have time to make it shorter.

My doctor recently described psychotherapy as "the slow boat to China," when compared to new techniques that are, allegedly, far more efficient. My mind was instantly whisked away to an exotic boat deck, under a full moon, with the sound of a waltz coming from the steamship's dining room; an alluring silhouette smoking by the railing, the scent of jasmine, brine, and elopement on the warm, subtropical breezes. For the first time in my life I'm now tempted to get therapy.

Those anxiety dreams in which you need to quickly go somewhere but can't find all your belongings — are they a symptom of modern life? Or did cavepeople have similar dreams, anxiously trying to get back to camp, with all the necessary pieces of the wooly mammoth they just killed, or all the ochre paints they so painfully collected? Perhaps even dogs and squirrels have such vexing oneiric experiences, concerning the frustrated retrieval of bones, or the eternally deferred collection of nuts.

I stumbled recently on a TV show called *Dolphins: Spy in the Pod*. This was a documentary that featured a camera hidden inside a fake, remote-controlled dolphin, which would then "spy" on the candid underwater activity of these highly intelligent sea creatures. This conceit hit me like a thunderbolt, since it finally explains those people that just seem to be *around,* or in the same room or space as you, but who don't really respond, or who are somehow a bit "off." Perhaps they are disguised cameras that the aliens are using to get close-up footage of our strange behavior. Possibly to watch while they eat dinner on their space sofas.

Few people realize that *Friends* was conceived as a modern remake of Buñuel's *Exterminating Angel*. It featured six random strangers who, because of some strange gypsy curse or uncanny supernatural force, could not go to any other coffee shop, in the whole of New York, than Central Perk, and could only leave their own apartments for very short periods. If one of these damned souls managed to speak to someone outside the group, or arrange a job that didn't involve the others — in other words, just as it looked like one of their lives would finally get on track — they would hear four quick claps from out of nowhere, and then suddenly find themselves, with a sense of profound horror, back on the couch in Central Perk, sipping a vanilla latte in 90s' mom jeans.

There should be a name (perhaps there already is?) for the belated meta-narcissism that can creep up on you mid-life, when you turn back to take a long and ongoing stock of where you are, and how you got there. I'm thinking of the kind so quintessentially captured and enacted by Proust, where the entire world is re-processed through the pinhole of one's singular psyche; inflected by love and infected by shame (and vice versa). A kind of conceited conatus, tipsy ipseity, and manual autopoieses all rolled into one. This should not be mistaken for vanity — though it can certainly succumb to such. But is rather a tribute to the ongoing, swiftly passing, fragile miracle of worlding, via the only aperture upon it that we know: ourselves.

Less than 1% of the world's knowledge survives today. The great classical philosophers we currently worship — the only ones to survive the amnesia of Time — shape our thoughts, our traditions, our politics: our very moral cores. And yet hardly any of them are mentioned in a compendium from the Golden Age itself, which instead sings the praises of thinkers who are lost to us, and who their own esteemed contemporaries rate much more highly. It's as if we founded an entire civilization around third-rate bands found in the vinyl bargain bins of a single thrift store, after the Library of Congress burned to the ground. That is to say, Socrates, Plato, and Aristotle were the Men Without Hats, Jamiroquai, and Maroon Five of their time. And tragically, we don't have a trace of the ancient Hellenic intellectual equivalent of Joni Mitchell, David Bowie, or Kendrick Lamar.

Chatroulette was such a lovely idea. Meeting random people from around the world and trying to start a conversation with them. It was almost Levinasian in its purity: confronting users with the ethical imperative embodied in the face of the Other, in all its vain pathos, generic presence, and singular vulnerability. The only problem is that Levinas — along with the makers of Chatroulette — did not anticipate the extent to which we would also be confronted with the *penis* of the Other, in all its veiny pathos, generic insistence, and singular culpability.

There is no point in accusing someone of being a "narcissist," since we are all narcissistic in one way or another. But I would like to make a distinction between the centrifugal and centripetal form of narcissism. The former describes a person who spins around their own ego in such a way that they fling their crap all over the place, and cover the walls with their own acrid, conatus-flavored spray. The latter revolves in the opposite direction, funneling the wider world *into* themselves, and folding its beckoning alterity into their own ever-evolving ego-crystal. Donald Trump is a centrifugal narcissist. Agnes Varda is a centripetal narcissist. Which would you rather be?

Sometimes I fancy being a reverse-therapist (or "inverse shrink"). My patients would arrive, lie on the couch, and start telling me all the things that they are excited about, all the ways they feel positive and affirmed and confident. About the many ways — both abstract and concrete — that life presents itself as worth living. About how profoundly content in their relationships they are. And about how little they blame their parents for anything.

Psychoanalytically inclined thinkers like to talk about "the Big Other." But what of "the little other"? This is someone who embodies all those who you look down upon, but whose recognition you need — albeit in homeopathic doses — in order to feel superior. Someone who, in your estimation, is lacking your maturity, wisdom, nuance, station, and so on. And yet, this impudent figure deigns to offer you advice, or treat you like a peer! Unlike the Big Other, who torments you with a sense of imposture and inadequacy, the little other exasperates, by refusing to acknowledge your genius.

The Nietzschean No* is as important as the Nietzschean Yes. In order to really affirm the vital mysteries, challenges, and energies of Life, you also need to avoid the parasitic, vampiric — and just plain boring and pointless — demands on your being.

So much of our internal monologue takes the form of, "If only X, then Y." But X will likely never happen. And even if it does, by then you will be thinking, "Now that I have X, I really need Y, in order to Z." Better then to shift the form to, "Given X, or the lack of X, how can I best dwell, or even thrive, in the Y of random Zness."

Social media is so addictive and powerful because it mimics the structure of the Big Other. So to say, it is an abstract, ubiquitous, and elusive form of attention from which we seek metaphysical recognition and validation. But this is also why it is so frustrating, depressing, and hollow. There is no Big Other. Just a multitude of little others, scrambling over each other's shoulders, dressed in a trench coat and a hat, pretending to be a grown up.

I've been trying to be more "zen" in general, which basically means breathing consciously and thinking twice before leaping head-first into the warm but treacherous waters of neurotic spirals. So while I was reading on the sofa just now, I smell that terrible jet fuel smell of whatever Americans squeeze on barbecue grills. Usually I would leap up, close the window, and then spend the next five minutes coming to terms with the

---

* Not to be confused with the Bartleby No, which tends toward the selfish and petty; jealously carving out more time to keep indulging in uncreative habits.

probability that my life has been shortened by at least a week. Instead, I took a few breaths, and watched myself begin to have this reaction. My brain, more sanguine than usual, then told itself, "ah, the smell of NYC rooftops in the summer! the people are enjoying this fine Sunday," and kept reading…. The moral of the story? Being more zen about stuff can make you put up with something that will probably kill you; or at least make you sick. But at least you feel more chill about it.

It must be exhausting being a young woman of a certain hue and class, since — from what I can gather, listening on the street — it seems mandatory to not only have a phone conversation with one's friend/lover/family member/etc., but then immediately call a different friend/lover/family member/etc. to relate and rehearse the entire conversation all over again. I'm amazed any of this demographic has any voice left, after so many conversations about conversations about previous conversations.

Sat next to a manspreader on the subway today, thereby sparking a conflict in the poor guy's body language. On the one hand, he wanted to press his leg against me to assert his alpha male dominance of the space. On the other hand, he was aware that this could be read as a homosexual come-on. So he oscillated between the two, clearly sickened by the predicament I had put him in.

New York City could be compared to those frightening fairy circles you read about as a child, in which a curious youth, walking through a forest, is seduced into a ring of magical, beckoning, glowing, lithe dancers. He or she whoops and hollers for what only seems like a few minutes, but is in fact a hundred years, back in the unenchanted "mortal" world. Eventually this person staggers out of what now appears to be only a ring of mushrooms: an exhausted old husk, without a human link to the real world left.

The first time I saw *Stalker* was when my dad took me to the cinema when I was nine years old. He told me it was science fiction, and I was in the height of my *Star Wars* obsession. I sat in the dark watching old, bald Russian men pontificating about art, suffering, and the futility of human existence in dripping tunnels for 90 minutes, before I finally snapped, and said very loudly, "Dad — I don't think there are going to be any robots. Can we go now?" To which he mercifully said yes.

When you think about it, a TV series is really just a movie that takes twenty-four hours to tell a story that should take only two.

What if we consider typos and random punctuation marks as stowaways in the text? Seeking passage? Shouldn't we somehow respect their desire to be smuggled away?

They say the early bird gets the worm. But that means the early worm gets eaten. So isn't this proverb really recommending that we sleep in late, just to be safe?

Love is just another name for infinite gratitude.

Single-cell organisms were the original life hack.

The self is an imaginary friend that we never grew out of.

Social media is just an updated version of "telling the bees."

In 2064, when the world has completely transformed into a *Mad Max*-style hellscape, the most precious form of currency — other than fresh water — will be USPS "forever stamps."

Shouldn't it be "print-on-request"? When did we all become so demanding?

If painters received peer-reviewed viewer reports, before exhibiting publicly:
VIEWER A: "Overall I found the treatment of the subject to be strong, but I felt there was too much yellow on the top right-hand corner. The brush-strokes seemed a little light at times. The choice of cavas size could even be described as inspired. The chimney sweep was beautifully rendered, although his face was obscured too much by shadow for my tastes. The painter should study dogs a lot more closely before attempting a spaniel like this one."
VIEWER B: "This painting is okay, but should really visually evoke some of my paintings if it wants to be taken seriously."

My superhero name is Worst-Case Scenario Man.

She's making a beeline
for the C line
in her A-line skirt.

Pity the poor butterfly, afraid to beat its wings for fear of the consequences.

LinkedIn: "You disappeared in 12 searches this week."

In the Old Imperial measuring system, a "chortle" describes the almost indiscernible difference between a snigger and a snicker?

In an unprecedented collaboration between CERN, NASA, the Académie française, and Moody's, it was found that everything in the universe is either underrated or overrated. *Not a single entity is rated precisely as it is, or deserves.**

Shouldn't it be uncritical mass?

Was anyone else, as a kid, bullied by their imaginary friend?

So-called "involuntary celibates" (incels) get all the media attention. But what about the "ambivalently debauched" (ambauches)?

I miss the simulation of democracy.

Gemeinschaft — the community you find yourself born into.
Geminecraft — the community you build inside a computer, in order to escape the community you were born into.

---

* "With the possible exception of Dante, Patagonia stock, Trader Joe's dark chocolate squares, walking on the beach at dusk, Juice Newton b-sides, and Tufts University."

Someone stole my thunder. And now I feel under-thundered. (Indeed, what a blunder — to ever-wonder how one can even become so sundered.)

Linguistic archaeologists, analyzing some of the earliest papyrus manuscripts, have discovered "sarcasm particles," which they describe as being "baked in" to human language from the beginning. This suggests that "snark," far from being a sign of intelligence, is actually a type of symbolic yeast infection, that we have all contracted from generations upon generations of communication interactions.

Hypothesis: the universe only invented bodies because it needed something to mechanically channel and sustain the cosmic breath, which floated around latent, and unrespirated, until fish and bears and people showed up.

People who live in stone houses shouldn't throw glasses.

Does any one else ever feel patronized by their own thoughts?

Just noticed my birthday suit is wrinkled.

You're all invited to my species-reveal party.

History Departments should change their program name to What People Managed To Do Before The Internet Studies.

Novels are incredibly low-def, and novelists rely on readers to fill in 90% of the worlds they are describing. Indeed, the reader should be getting a good share of the royalties for all that imaginative labor.

Approximately half of media studies is just reminding people — over and over — that a screen is not a window.

Rabbits fall down rabbit holes all the time, and they don't feel the need to go on about it.

Microdoucheing: the practice of interacting with obnoxious asshats as little as possible, each day.

Bruno Latour left the bosom of a famous, wealthy wine-making family to become a scholar and theorist. I am happy to go in the opposite direction, if someone knows the secret of doing so.

Imagine the world we might be living in, if Central Park featured a Rabelais Garden.

In the mid-'90s, for a brief moment, I was a raver. Now I'm just a ranter.

New Yorkers, recomposing their tired features in the mirror each morning, into the shape of a Do Not Disturb sign.

Yes, "ghosting" someone is a form of violence. But by the same token, going ghosthunting is just as cruel. Make peace with your absent poltergeist, and move on.

According to Agamben, the Romans invented the figure of *homo sacer* so that anyone may legally kill anyone else who can't figure out how to use a Doodle Poll.

Nothing illustrates the homogenizing effect of globalization more than the Netflix special series. No matter what country it is from, it has gone through the same filters: conceptually, ideologically, and technically. They all look the same, even if some of the noses and languages are somewhat different.

That feeling when you're being simultaneously under-utilized and over-extended.

Motion to recognize Teflon Tuesday — one day a week in which we all collectively resolve not to let any of the bullshit tornado get under our skin.

Academia: where speaking slowly is equated with being more intelligent.

Wondering if there is a market for anti-natalist children's literature.

Dolly 1.0: "It costs a lot of money to look this cheap."
Dolly 2.0: "It costs a lot of money to clone this sheep."

Akrasiastasis: the perverse tendency of collective institutions supposedly dedicated to the public good, entropically ensuring that the catastrophic status quo is retained at any cost. See *The New York Times* and *The Guardian*.

More often than not, pride is just insecurity wearing a suit.

At Harvard, university professors are the only class of faculty allowed to graze their cattle on Harvard Yard. At the New School, they are the only group allowed to graze their emotional support animals on the green roof.

In class yesterday, we decided that ghosts are an instance of trans-dimensional FOMO, in which departed spirits jealously try to avoid missing out on Life.

Heterobiblioaffectundrum: the nagging knowledge that you can never find the right book to match the right mood.

Max Weber's less known sequel, *The Catholic Shirk Ethic*

Helicopters flying by like
        jackhammers in the sky
                reducing my peace to rubble.

Tinder, but for someone to water your plants when you're away.

When nature calls, you urinate.
When culture calls, you ruminate.

TODAY'S HOROSCOPE

Aries: someone who has been making your life difficult will extend a literal olive branch; which will make taking the elevator very awkward.

Leo: you will be plagued by the same pebble in your shoe, even after tipping it out into a canal.

Gemini: while reading on the subway, a brony will offer you a stick of gum.

Cancer: while waiting for the bus in the rain, you will be convinced that Totoro is standing right next to you. But when you turn to look, you will realize that it's actually Cliff, the it guy.

Taurus: you will exchange a knowing look with Brian Eno, when you recognize him in an airport lounge.

Virgo: minutes before your afternoon nap, a phone call will inform you that you have just been nominated for the Nobel Prize for Pornography.

Libra: after several failed attempts, you will successfully patent a new kind of onion, that makes people laugh when they cut into it.

Scorpio: a beautiful stranger will give you what appears to be a treasure map, scribbled on the back of a perfume sample.

Sagittarius: in the midst of overwhelming evidence, you will finally admit that we live in a totalitarian society.

Capricorn: you will stifle a sneeze the entire work-day, only to explode into a thousand tiny pieces, the moment you get home.

Aquarius: that strange smell emanating from the fridge crisper draw will begin to also whisper your name.

Pisces: you will ignore three phone calls from your mother.

Oxymoron of the day: "curated experience."

Dear Professor.
I write to invite you to present your researches at the Second Annual Conference on Intellectual Topics Concerning Cultural Directions in New Media Technology Innovations and Critique. The inviting committee were impressed by the article you published fifteen years ago on a totally unrelated topic. This conference will be in Hawaii, for some reason, cost hundreds of dollars to register for, and we will provide all participants with a laminated Certificate of Attendance and a tote bag.
Please do not contact us if you have any questions.
Signed,
The Organizing Committee

Geese are incredibly efficient animals, semiotically speaking. With one single letter — the letter V — they manage to communicate the message: "It's freezing! Time to get the fuck out of here!"

Most people know about the Stoics. But few people have heard of the Hysterics: a group of philosophers from Crete, around the 3rd century BCE, who believed that we should face existence with as much drama as possible; dwelling on worst-case scenarios, resenting roads not taken, and exhibiting an ethical commitment to generally blowing everything out of proportion.

Humans think in binary because we have two hands. ("On one hand X, but on the other hand Y.") Whereas octopi, for instance, can think in octonary. No doubt their philosophy is all the richer for it.

Don't let douche nozzles get under your brain knickers.

Dominic Pettman: offering media-poor content to the world since 1985.

My good friend, Scam Likely, has a terrible time trying to convince people to answer her calls.

American spelling can be very strange. For instance, they spell "corruption" as "l-o-b-b-y-i-n-g."

Scientists seek the precise point where resentment crystallizes into delusion.

Examples of American Socialism:
- Public Libraries
- GI Bill
- Community College
- Free Lunch Program
- Traveling Pants

We have FedEx minds and USPS hearts.

Is there anything less rational than rational choice theory.

Most of us feel (and fear) we missed The Memo. While others act as if they were the privileged ones who did. But guess what: *there is no memo.*

Death is the only thing that truly takes one's breath away.

We talk about something being "harmless" when we mean ineffective. The implication is that one cannot be effective without causing harm.

What to do when your revenue stream becomes an income trickle?

Red wine, as the name suggests, is inherently communist, and yearns to be free.

Sometimes I love people, but hate humanity. Other times, it's the other way around.

Feelings are overrated.
(While sensations are underrated.)

TED Talk ontology: It's turtle-necks, all the way down.

"Human Resources" is an admission that contemporary labor is (still) all about extraction.

Design Within Retch

I prefer to philosophize with a hammer dulcimer.

My doctor has diagnosed me with advanced acedia.
He's old school like that.

Why won't anyone keep me in the manner I'm accustomed?

I still find it strange that Mexico has a national holiday to celebrate mayonnaise.

The Turin Test.
In which you whip a robot horse in an Italian square, and see if anyone has a nervous breakdown.

Top scientists remind nation that less is *not* in fact more.
Indeed, it is precisely less than more. (Which is why it is called "less.")

Medieval knights often had a faithful retainer, who was there to ensure that their master's teeth stayed in place.

One of the main functions of ideology is to act as a machine that produces widespread and contagious underreactions from the general public.

If we were to remove the word "precisely," Jenga-style, from the world, the entire edifice of Continental Philosophy would collapse.

Do you need more doors? Come down to Mordor More Doors Warehouse. We'll give you more doors. For less!

Swine-Pearl Productions

Every time something in me dies, a friend succeeds.

I've given up my quest for the last laugh, and am now settling for the third-to-last chortle.

This Coital Mortal

20th — century of the self
21st — century of the selfie
22nd — century of the shellfish

Publishing is a perfect example of cruel optimism.
("Maybe they will read *this* one.")

Manhattan was the first Manhattan Project.

Few people realize that "yike" is the singular of "yikes." Most occasions that now prompt the response "yikes" were judged worth only a "yike" in the 18th century, for example. Such is the way of linguistic inflation.

"The precariat" actually sounds like an optimistic, relatively secure, name for what most workers are experiencing these days.

The best reason to have a kid, as far as I can tell, is to stop focusing on your own mommy and/or daddy issues, and start passing these on to someone else.

One thing that meditation has taught me: one's deepest fears and anxieties live and breed in the invisible brine that exists in the fleeting, infinite space following the end of an exhalation, and before the next breath begins.

Nationalities exist purely to name a specific type of stupidity. For instance, there is a particularly American, French, Australian, or Chinese way to manifest human stupidity. (Of course the same goes for embodying and enacting different species of genius. But sadly these are much less common.)

Scientists unveil new electron microscope, capable of discovering hundreds of hitherto unknown microaggressions.

Drink. Prey. Lust.

Buddhist 20-minute silent TED talk

The hegemony of pornography has all but eclipsed the erotic.

The irony of being ironic is that ultimately there is no meaningful difference between the one who enjoys a cultural artifact naively, and the one who does so while winking at the world.

Two things you don't want to encounter while on holiday: mozzies and Aussies.

Cicadas are nature's white noise machine.

Airbnb host, at this remote cabin in the Italian woods:

"This is key for the gate, this is button for the AC, this is remote for the TV.... Please put recycling here. And remember, don't let the man with the homemade pig mask into house, when he knocks on the door."

The French government announces that it will no longer be making any new shrugs. Instead they will be outsourcing the production of shrugs to China. The French, appalled by this latest move, begin a grassroots, country-wide shrug recycling campaign.

Everything will be fine. And when it is not fine, I will make it fine, by being fine with what is not fine.

"But mom — it was only a few pages!"
"Now young lady. You *know* that Deleuze is a gateway drug to Laruelle."

Imagine how interesting our ideas might be, if they weren't already wing-clipped by preemptive defensiveness, and the anticipation of heading off critique.

Life hacks
#1: If your supermarket is out of kale, incite a revolution and seize the means of production.
#2: If you're awkward at parties, convince humanity to commit *en masse* to the voluntary mass extinction movement.

A homeless guy got on to the subway yesterday, and said to himself, in a very loud voice: "Oh no. This is one of those *passenger* trains."

'Tis the season in Central Park when blushing brides sprout out of the ground like pale spring tubers.

As the weather gets warmer, I start to suspect that I'm just playing an extra in a vast and elaborate theme park catering to European tourists.

A small child babbling to her father on the way to school. He nods along distracted, thinking about Karen from work.

On beautiful mornings like this, I run around the park — at a slow walking pace — and then have breakfast.

Sometimes I like to confuse and exasperate the bird-watchers in Central Park by hiding in the bushes, and blowing rare bird-calls through special Chinese mail-order avian whistles.

Buying raw milk from the back of a truck in Manhattan is a bit like a drug deal in *Breaking Bad,* except instead of guns and gangsters you find tote bags and yoga moms.

New York is just as dangerous for the wallet as it was in 1975. Only now you are likely to get robbed not by a hoodlum with a knife, but by an organic farmer with a forced grin and credit card swiper attached to his iPhone.

Museum-grade douche nozzles brobaking on the roof deck opposite.

New York is about *intensity* of life (and not at all quality of life).

Lots. Of naps. Till Brooklyn!

The coffee in New York is immeasurably better than when I arrived, fifteen years ago. But at what cost?!

Who wants to go on my Central Park tour: "Birding for Aging Punks"?

Walked past a salad-bar-restaurant-concept BS thing downtown, with "architectural" highline-type seating, filled with yoga pants start-up people with dead eyes, munching on kale as if it were joyless crack. We're truly living in a bad mashup of *Soylent Green, Stepford Wives, Nathan Barley, Perfect,* and *They Live.*

Who will save Central Park from the Central Park Conservancy?

The EPA has yet to determine the amount of pollution caused in Manhattan each year by invisible plumes of privilege.

A young mother to her four-year old son on the subway yesterday: "You need to be more solution-oriented."

The cyclist's attitude toward pedestrians mirrors the driver's attitude toward cyclists. There is a timeless political lesson here.

An old guy jogged past me wearing a "Running Sucks" t-shirt. When he saw me smile he gasped and winced: "I really mean it!"

Just as a certain temperature threshold releases a cloud of cicadas into the air, 80 degrees in NYC automatically triggers plumes of Latin dance music into the atmosphere.

Sometimes I wish I lived in Yonkers, so I would have occasion to say "Yonkers" more often.

For around 30 years, you wonder when life is really going to start. Then, practically overnight, you start wondering when your life stopped moving forward. Which means, I suppose, that for about ten minutes you really were living.

A mass shooshing broke out in the main branch of the New York Public Library yesterday. Eight egos were hurt.

"I'm sorry, the other customers are complaining, so I'm going to have to ask you to be less Australian."

I'm tired of buskers singing "Imagine" and "Jealous Guy" at Strawberry Fields. So I may sit on a bench with an upturned hat and just say "Number 9, Number 9, Number 9" over and over again.

Competitive Motherhood.
Today's big matchup: Park Slope vs. the Upper-West Side.
Place your bets please…

Just watched two different couples walk into a juice store, all four of them wearing Canada Goose coats. I'm almost certain they left with the wrong partner, without even realizing it.

Sheep Meadow in Central Park is, on a fine day, still full of sheep.

A tourist couple, with poor English, came up to me in Central Park today. I couldn't work out why they were trying to find a "dead beetle." Then I realized that they were looking for the John Lennon memorial at Strawberry Fields.

If you listen really carefully, while walking through the park, you can hear the screams of agony coming from the daffodils, as they scorch in the unseasonably fierce sunlight.

Must NYC be a magnet for douche nozzles?

Indecent Proposal (Central Park edition): "I'll give you a million dollars for your dog."

After five weeks away, I've lost my immunity to New York's ridiculous prices. I keep arguing with cashiers.

Once upon a time, tourists came to New York to gawp at the concentrated vision of The Future it embodied. Now it serves more as a museum for, and abject lesson against, what happens when you siphon money away from public infrastruture.

Vintage pornography now circulates in the pubic domain.

Is a shit-ton somehow different to a regular ton?

Forsaken (adj.) — the state of being abandoned, bereft.
Foresaken (adj.) — the sense that one is *about* to be abandoned, bereft.

In the American remake of *Black Mirror,* Steve Carell plays the President who, instead of enduring the humiliation of having sex with a pig on live TV, is instead obliged to give an intern health insurance.

I just finished watching *The Martian*. If I wanted to watch an unpleasant man eat a potato every day, then I'd prefer to watch Bela Tarr's *Turin Horse*.

If Hitchcock made *Rear Window* today, it would just feature twenty or so people, lying in bed and staring at their phones.

The *Mad Max* films are as close as Australia will get to neo-realism.

Who knew that being something of a cinephile would help me communicate with a French doctor?
Doctor: "Quels sont votre symptômes?"
Me: "À bout de souffle."

I'm looking forward to the 3D IMAX version of Ozu's *Tokyo Story*.

Why Are They Now?
A new TV show dedicated to addressing the existential conundrum of a different celebrity each week.

I imagine the Rebel Alliance in *Star Wars* paid for all those fancy spaceships with an NPR-style pledge drive.

Family Freud
A new game show in which two different families compete to connect common phrases to Oedipal dramas.

Why will none of the big studios respond to my movie pitch: "Manic Pixie Dream Girl vs. Depressive Elfin Nightmare Boy"?

Watching Marie Kondo to avoid tidying up.

A TV show, *à la Queer Eye,* in which Adorno, Angela Davis, Basho, and Simone Weil make interventions into the lives of shallow urbanites.

Fox's early reality TV show, *When Good Times Go Bad,* was originally going to be called, *Gadzooks! Peripeteia!*

The distance between Ricky Gervais and David Brent isn't as significant as Ricky Gervais thinks it is.

Clem's Knee
A remake of Rohmer's famous film, but with two construction workers.

A new TV show called *Occam,* about a detective who defends himself against thugs with a straight razor, and always catches and convicts the most obvious suspect.

Most films from the 1940s seem less "dated" than most TV shows from the 1980s.

Occam's Razor — the principle of selecting the answer that makes the fewest assumptions, when presented with competing hypothetical possibilities.
Dominic's Spatula — the principle of doing the least amount of changes, or making the least amount of effort, in order to avoid complicating life, but still have it running more or less smoothly.

At court, Kurt would curtly and covertly curtsy as a courtesy.

Shostakovich was accosted in Costco over a costly churro.

Only during blizzards do wizards eat lizard gizzards.

It is inappropriate to appropriate the prostrate apostate's prostate.

Say hello to a phalanx of fellows whose phallophilia lies fallow on the hollow feather pillow.

Pop-up one-stop mom-and-pop popcorn and popsicle shop.

The brazen brass brasserie boasted a bevy of bruised Bruces wearing bronze brassieres.

I was so precocious that I had a *L'Eclisse* lunch box in the fifth grade.

The *Network* remake for 2018 finishes with a desultory speech: "I'm mad as hell!… And I'm gonna just keep on taking it."

Few people are aware that *Halt and Catch Fire* is based on a 16th-century illuminated manuscript — entitled *Cease Ye and Combust* — which detailed the invention of the printing press.

Negative epiphany listening to a Giallo music mix: the reason I find Quentin Tarantino's movies so off-putting is that his obsessive recreational instincts are all well and good for a pastiche of style, but the very attention to detail drains the thing of the spirit it's trying so desperately to channel. In trying to lovingly replicate the loose and perverse joy of a trashy '70s exploitation film, he banishes all joy from his own work.

Many tribal cultures do not consider their members full-grown adults until they have seen thirty-four summers — the age at which one starts truly appreciating Barbara Stanwyck movies.

Yesterday I watched a beautiful print of Jean Grémillon's *Lady Killer* (*Geule d'Amour*, 1937). It would make a great triple feature, along with *Blue Angel* and *That Obscure Object of Desire*. The main character, played by Jean Gabin, seemed to misunderstand the film he was in, as if insisting on the hidden melodramatic stakes behind the light Lubitschesque touch. He could not heed the worldly advice of his lover's mother: "Life is for living. Everyone deserves some happiness. Only the selfish don't share."

One thing that the whole Trump situation tells me is that when I went to see *Back to the Future,* as a young lad, almost half the theater was silently rooting for Biff.

So You Think You Can Dane
(a competition reality show that pits potential Hamlets against one another)

Press Release, ABC Studios, for immediate release:
In order to keep things fresh and interesting for our loyal viewers, *Dancing with the Stars will* now be offering a bold new format. This coming season we will feature one star per week, performing solo for 21 whole minutes, commercial-free. The judges will be asking our stars to use their bodies to express either an unresolved conflict in their own lives, or a personal response to troubling world events. Episode One will feature Billy Ray Cyrus, and his interpretation of intergenerational ambivalence, to the haunting ambient music of Joanna Brouk; and Episode Two will feature Tori Spelling, and her somatic exegesis of the conflict in Yemen to a symphony by György Ligeti. As always, your hosts will be Tom Bergeron and Erin Andrews.

Is there a name for that thing when a film, say, ostensibly satirizes or attacks something, but is in fact wallowing in and perpetuating said target? I'm thinking of films like *Donnie Darko, Requiem for a Dream,* or *Fight Club.*

In hindsight, *Jackass* was a clear warning sign of impending Trumpetry.

Why do all the different planets in the *Star Wars* galaxy look like parts of Earth?

No thanks to *The Good Place,* we'll soon have to deal with a generation of misguided souls who have the absurd — and quintessentially American — notion that philosophy is about "being a good person."

Pitch for a retro-grindhouse horror flick — *Death Drive In* — where 1970s teens are locked in a drive-in movie theater, and terrorized by a sadist, called Thanatos, who looks like a Greek Sigmund Freud.

Moving pictures had a good run. But after watching *Vox Lux,* I think it's time to call the whole thing off. Time to go back to lithographs, puppet shows, and *tableaux vivants.*

I still think The Situation is possibly the greatest name in history.

The Wilhelm Scream will outlast humanity.

You should all subscribe to my YouTube channel, in which I film myself reacting to reaction videos.

"Facebook Denies That It Shared User Data with Eye of Sauron."

Which is the bigger deal-breaker, when it comes to meeting a prospective Tinder date?
1) They have less than 1k followers on Twitter
2) They don't even have a podcast

The human race will be followed by the post-human interview, analysis, and press conference.

Everything happens for a reason. Usually a stupid or terrible reason.

Honey is the message. It wants to convey nothing but sweetness.

The best way to feel ten pounds lighter is to lose ten pounds.

A Tolstoy cover band called Vronsky Beat.

If someone who ruins a scene by overacting is called a "ham," what do we call someone who ruins a scene by *underacting*? A tofu?

I'll show you my mid-life crisis if you show me yours.

The moral of every movie ever: don't get involved.

I would like to be a xenomusicologist.

Zenophobia: the fear of arriving at your destination.

The difference of minor narcissisms.

One of the biggest mistakes in life is to take it personally.

Central Paris is an ongoing bourgeois cosplay convention.

When I see an old, grizzled man at a bar, I assume he has WWII stories to tell, or something equally Old Timey. But in truth, given the actual chronology involved, he is more likely to tell me about the time he got laid during a Jethro Tull concert.

In the middle ages, women were burnt at the stake for organizing unauthorized rituals, talking to animals, or publishing with Zero Books before tenure.

To seduce without the aid of magic potions.
#nophiltre

Two of the most transcendent albums of the millennium so far — Björk's *Vespertine* and Joanna Newsom's *Have One On Me* — were both inspired by male (erm) "muses": Matthew Barney and Andy Samberg, respectively. Ample evidence that the inspiration of love has pretty much nothing to do with the beloved!

As a rule, I'm against marriage. But I love weddings!

Judging by the conversations I hear on the streets of New York, two thirds of the young women of this city consistently fail the Bechdel Test.

THE HUMID CONDITION

To fall out of love is to render the former beloved back to a simple piece of the global jig-saw puzzle; rather than representing the image to which all the other pieces previously combined to reveal.

I have Tinder feelings towards you.

Love conquers all. Especially the lovers.

That time Bill Clinton came out as a Lacanian: "I did not have sexual relations with that woman."

Marriage proposal:
Let's take this organic attraction, and make it a paranoid and tyrannical bourgeois unit.

This bus is full of noisy children. Or as I like to call them, The Residues of Eros.

Both my data plan and dating plan involve rollover minutes.

I like my women like I like avant-garde dance: beautiful, but confusing.

Five incoherent demands of the other while making love:
1) recognize and worship my individuality
2) insult and disavow my individuality
3) save me from the burden of being (a being)

4) deliver me from the fear of death (through the act of symbolic sacrifice)
5) make me immortal

There are few places lonelier than the libido. Which is why we are not so much looking for our desires to be satisfied, but rather shared.

In the future, thanks to brain-to-brain neural networks and face-matching algorithms, we will know when someone is having a sexual fantasy about us, and then we can either charge them for the pleasure, or sue them for breach of copyright.

In the future, when androids are indistinguishable from humans, we may fall in love with someone, marry them, and then suddenly discover they are a spam bot. Until the divorce comes through, we will be legally obliged to listen to them talk about a specific brand all day every day.

Sex is very lazy. You're essentially outsourcing masturbation to someone else.

Spare a thought for trisexuals.

The lover's economy: "I love you, so you owe me. But don't pay me back in one go. Rather, pay me in installments, over time."

Maybe Lacanians are just bad lovers. (Or bad lovers become Lacanians.)

Most cases of misogyny are really instances of gynophobia.

Refuse to be reduced to a sex object. But consider being elevated to one, on special occasions.

Masturbation = intracourse

I love you!*

We have the capacity to destroy each other merely by kissing, or even flirting, with another person. Fourier was the only person to seriously attempt to lessen this destructive power.

You would think that having love handles would actually help, rather than hinder, when it comes to being "picked up" in public.

Seize the means of seduction!

Marriage: taking sociality to degree zero, so one can be alone in company.

Of course we all love to sing along with the classic Carole King song, "You make me feel…you make me feel you make me feel like a socially constructed heavily gendered subject position…. (oooooh, you make me feel so *reified*)…"

---

* Terms and conditions apply.

Experts estimate that over 91% of people are over-cathecting.

"I'm not heterosexual. I'm alt.straight."

Abject wealth and obscene poverty.

The French World Cup team has three players sidelined due to injury, and two because of ennui.

Dominic's razor: always choose the option in which it is most likely that you will be able to eat cheese.

Carpe diem is an old fisherman's saying, meaning "seize the carp."

French birds love Popol Vuh.

Scientists discover a "quantum coo state," in which — for a rare and fleeting moment — both lovers are fully and objectively determined to be Schmoopie.

Daguerre invented the first photograph when a saucy shop girl said to him, "Why don't you take a picture, mister? It'll last longer!"

"It's just common knowledge. Like hotels near train stations are seedy, or crows are the restless reincarnated souls of defrocked priests."

Life was uncomfortable for Gordon, having been born with a silver spoon in his mouth, a frog in his throat, a thorn in his side, a chip on his shoulder, a weight on his chest, a fire in his belly, a monkey on his back, a bee in his bonnet, a flea in his ear, an apple in his eye, and a stick up his butt.

Wait. You mean "influencer" isn't just a fancy new word for hypnotist?

Broke: "I'm gonna put a cap in your ass."
Woke: "I'm gonna screen-cap your ass."

2019: The year anxiety became a competitive sport.

Course Outline:
In this course we will be re-enacting the famous Chomsky–Foucault debate on human nature through the medium of puppetry. We will use puppets as a "material" means to reflect on such matters as:
- the nature of televised debates;
- the specific cultural and historical context of televised European erudition;
- the afterlives of mythologized moments in the persistence of Theory, both in and beyond the academy;
- the character of multi-lingual encounters and events;
- the embodied affect and somatic protocols of intellectual exchange;
- the power of orange juice as social lubricant;
- the ambient influence of random bearded dudes in yellow turtlenecks.

This course bears 4 credits, and is a companion course to Spinoza's Ethics as Adapted for the Art of Mime.

Usually, writing for me is like chasing a tiger. I can see the tail of what I really want to say, but I never really catch up with it. This tiger is forever hiding in the long grass of the next sentence.

Lana del Rey is what happened when Tumblr became sentient.

If you have a terrible secret, and you never want a soul to discover it, then I suggest you publish it in an edited hardcover-only anthology from Routledge.

Sometimes I worry that I'm allergic to nouns.

Deleuze is academic ayahuasca.

<u>The Salad Bar</u>
Devotees of the cruel goddess Kale
form an orderly line, pale
and patient;
dreaming of distant yoga vacations
while refilling flat stomachs
in joyless ingestion stations;
opening the tired and puckered sluices
from a bottomless well of
sump-colored ten-dollar juices.

There's a sound here in the French countryside that's hard to tell if it's a close blowfly or a distant cow. Hard to tell whether it's a low buzzing or a buzzy lowing.

It is said that when the human race emerged from the others, a certain quota of spirit and intelligence was put aside for this new, ambitious animal. Unfortunately, as its numbers multiplied and mushroomed — 1 billion, 2 billion, 6 billion, 20 billion — the same amount of spirit and intelligence was available, leading to a great dilution of their souls and achievements.

Tempted to start sowing my classes with white lies; such as: pine trees are so called because our ancestors believed they pined for god, which is why the wind sounds so melancholy through their needles, and they grow so straight, toward heaven.

Creeper vines are terrifying monsters, ready to strangle and devour anything in its path. But the process is too slow for our eyes to notice. So we merely consider them picturesque embellishments.

A "molecule" is a very very small mole.
#TheMoreYouKnow

I just received my orgone donor card in the mail.

"I don't dance. But I do move my body rhythmically with vigor."
(Something I said in my dream last night.)

When being introduced to someone, in a professional or formal context, I like to shake hands firmly, and say, in a confident voice, "I'm allowed to be here."

If I were Icarus, I would likely stick to doing some gentle loops a few feet above the ground, and aim for the shade, just in case.

Beware the ideas of March.

T-shirt: "I'm not your teachable moment."

Oxymoron of the day: self-regulation

Oxymoron of the next day: fashion sense

Pokémon Go, but for course releases.

Cartoon:
A personified label maker is sitting at a bar, clearly already drunk. He's drawling to the bartender: "I just get so tired of putting a label on everything."

Spring hopes internal

The original "public sphere" and "private sphere" are made out of a titanium and platinum alloy. For over a century they were stored in a temperature-controlled vault, under the streets of Paris — mostly for verification purposes — but were both stolen in late 1970s — many suspect by the Deep State.

Was Huey Lewis's news fake?

NEW OLYMPIC SPORTS BEING INTRODUCED NEXT CYCLE

Knitting
Meditation
Networking
Home brewing
Speed reading
Long distance dating
Tunneling
Synchronized astronomy
Wheedling
Sledging
Kvetching
Pokémon Go
400 meters flirting
Selfie relay
Goat dressage
Ice taxidermy
Mine hurdling
Table setting
Turntablism
ted talks
Nostalgia
Doubt
Pole dancing
Dog curbing
Critical media theory

If short shorts are "hotpants," then does that make normal shorts "lukewarm pants"?

Australia has a vista point called Captain Cook Lookout. When I was a kid, my parents told me it was named after the last words he ever heard.

Ignorance breeds contempt.
Familiarity breeds contempt.
What I'm saying is: there's no shortage of contempt to go round.

That thing where you string up a dream catcher on your porch, but then forget to check it for a month, and you realize it caught some dreams that you didn't clean out, which explains that rather rancid smell that comes and goes, but you don't really have the stomach to face a trapped and half-rotting dream, so you just sort of quickly move it into the supply closet while holding your nose, and then go about your daily business, hoping the rapidly decomposing dream doesn't seep into your nightmares.

The sixth sense is actually the one that helps you inherently feel precisely the invisible line, about forty feet from the beach, that you shouldn't cross while topless.

Art project:
Since humans are very unlikely to be around in a hundred years or so, what are we to do about all those lost literary legacies? How do we salvage Shakespeare, Dante, and indeed our own humble jottings, from complete oblivion? My answer:

teach cockroaches to read. Please donate to the CLP (Cockroach Literacy Project).

Art project:
Sell the black, gnawing, hollow existential void at the heart of all Instagram activity on eBay.

Sometimes life throws us lemons, and all we can make is a kind of unsweetened lemon juice concoction.

I sincerely hope there is a vulgar Mexican drag queen out there somewhere called Kweef Latina.

Someone needs to map the Beyoncé/Shakira international date line.

To live in a place where the months can be counted by the color of butterflies.

Salt of the earth vs pepper of the sky.

Tree of knowledge vs the rubber plant of ignorance.

I'm more of a shaker than a mover.

A little bit of marzipan goes a long way. And none at all goes even further.

Californians tend to wear their genitals on their sleeve.

The echoes of Hellenic mythology reverberate around today's Italian beach towns: "Vedo la medusa!"

Vacation: when you spend thousands of dollars and travel thousands of miles to worry about the same things you always worry about at home.

The universal freemasonry of bored teenagers on holiday with their parents.

Life is a near-death experience.

Humans are the animal that cannot live in the here and now.

Humanity began the moment a bonobo said out loud: "You have brought shame to this family!"

In France, *Where's Waldo* features a woman, rather than a man, and is called *Cherchez la Femme*.

Air France: where your deep-seated fears and nagging anxieties travel with you for free.

I'm not selfish enough to have kids.

Airports are a shiny reminder that capital thinks of us nothing more than squishy, anonymous, and docile creatures that excrete money when squeezed.

The skeptical dupe.
For instance, someone who will buy and install Alexa in their home, in order to write a column about how our privacy is being eroded by technologies like Alexa.

It appears that my waistline has become a waistsphere.

If a seashell puts a human up to its ear, it can hear the sound of Fox News.

I don't think I've ever met a Sagittarius? Do they even exist? Or is it something they quickly invented to finish the Zodiac before a looming deadline?

A good marriage allows you to be alone, without being lonely. A bad one, you are lonely, but never alone.

Show me your emoji history, and I will show you who you are.

I met History the other day, strolling through the municipal gardens, and eventually summoned up enough courage to ask if I could take a picture. She said, "Very well, young man. But not from over there. That's my wrong side."

From this day forward, wine shall be known only by its true and ancient name: "coping juice."

The Bluebeard fable is clearly an allegory about man's fear that his good lady wife will discover his porn collection.

I frequently write occasional pieces.

Adjuncts are like academic session musicians. If only they were paid as well.

Happy faculties are all alike; every unhappy faculty is unhappy in its own way.

All my books go several directions at once. So I've never really written a monograph. Rather, a series of polygraphs.

That thing where you compose the world's most glowing letter of recommendation, in your mind, while walking home from the subway… for yourself.

I get a tiny microdose of pleasure whenever I write, "Or by appointment," after my office hours. It makes me feel a little bit like the Queen.

I would never attend a conference that accepted one of my papers.

We should all have a shadow CV for articles and books we would have *liked* to write, but don't have the time or will to do so.

I had dinner with a professor friend last night in a French bistro in the West Village. As we stood up to leave, the woman dining alone next to us said (in a broad working-class Boston accent): "Excuse me, are you both teachers?… I mean, college teachers?" We admitted that we were. To which she smiled and said, earnestly: "Thank you for your service!" We left the place feeling like newly decorated heroes.

White men invented academia when they figured that there simply *must* be a way to get paid for publicly expressing disdain or disappointment with literally everyone else's theories, ideas, and communication skills.

Starting next month, I have decided to start charging "convenience fees" for things like answering email messages, showing up for meetings, grading papers, paying bills, listening to tangential anecdotes without falling asleep, giving way to others on the side-walk, etc. I trust that you will understand.

The question haunting every encounter with an academic. Did I just talk to an interesting person? Or a boring person, in the possession of interesting information?

Why settle for a paramour, when you could have a metamour?

DeGrader™ — an app that helps find people nearby to do my grading for me.

At a certain point, the man of letters (gender intended), turns from the works that first entranced him, to the hagiographies of those who produced them.

People who doubt that academia offers an exciting and exotic lifestyle need look no further than our photos on social media. Here, you will see a heart-skipping panorama of badly dressed people standing in groups, sitting in groups, hunched over papers, milling about catering tables, staring unblinking at the camera like owls trapped in fluorescent-lit beige boxes, holding microphones, standing behind podiums, and covered in glowing bullet-points from badly projected PowerPoint presentations.

Perhaps it's time to start including a "Works Not Cited" section, for books that are either 1) over-rated; 2) over-cited; 3) relevant, but not helpful; 4) helpful, but not relevant; 5) too long; 6) written by a friendly nemesis; 7) written by someone with a better job than you; 8) written by someone who patronized you during a conference panel Q&A session; 9) really, much too much too long; 10) something you've already relied on too often; 11) published by a predatory press.

It would save a lot of time if we all agreed to using a rubber stamp of a smiling glowworm, with a speech bubble simply saying, "Glowing Review!" for friends, ex-students, colleagues, etc.

Socrates: the original mansplainer.

As Confucius once said, "you get the administrative appointment you deserve."

Symposia — an opportunity for people to talk past each other, in the same room.

The other conference participants wondered why Pandora refused to open her lunch box.

In academia, there are more initiatives launched every day than there are people to respond to, or be influenced by, them. Indeed, I suspect there are more academic initiatives than there are academics.

Academicworld: a place not overly unlike Westworld, where young people pay upward of 30k a year to interact with "hosts" programmed to deliver the same "experience," year after year after year.

Math, biology, physics, etc. are considered the "hard sciences." So I think we should start referring to economics, sociology, anthropology, etc. as the "easy sciences."

Not many people know that the practice of footnotes began in ancient Egypt, when scholars would write references on their own feet, or the feet of obliging students, during a severe papyrus shortage.

"You have asked about my relationship with the candidate for tenure: I have only met Professor X on four hundred different occasions. We first met at a conference, and exchanged a few emails about the possibility of co-editing a special journal issue, which subsequently became an alibi for late breakfasts in hotel beds, romantic balloon journeys over Cappadocia, impassioned arguments over cocktails in Hanoi, robbing a bank together in Durban, and co-teaching a series of political workshops in a seedy Lisbon café. I don't believe that any of these interactions hampers my capacity to be objective in my assessment of the candidate's dossier."

Seems not one of my students remembered to tip me this year.

Zeno's manuscript: a draft that you write, edit, cut in half, and rewrite so many times that it never hits the bookshelves.

Soon enough students will rate every class as ☺ or ☹ or 😐 on an official University app, called TeechGood, at the end of each session.

If I were rich, I would offer a dozen "fallowships" every year, in which successful applicants would enjoy a year of rest and respite, doing nothing but pondering and pottering about, with absolutely no pressure or expectation of producing something at the end. Indeed, no projects are allowed, and any books or other tangible artifacts emerging from this hiatus from life — this time of fruitfully fruitless reflection — are sternly frowned upon.

Volume 1: Hegel Today
Volume 2: Hegel Yesterday
Volume 3: Hegel A Couple of Years Ago, After that Bad Break Up with Heather

Coarse evaluations.

IN MY PARALLEL UNIVERSE

Teenagers wake before dawn, put on their club gear, and go birding in the park together in large, contemplative groups.

Graphic designers, branding experts, and hedge-fund managers skulk around the Staples parking lot, waiting for a flat-bed truck to come by, and a Latino man to lean out of the passenger side window and say, "you... you... and you. Get in. We have a job across town."

Old people become radiantly beautiful just before they die, like autumn leaves.

Business men in pin-striped suits totter to work in high heels.

Ingmar Bergman was born as a Brazilian woman, and made light-hearted films about Catholic insouciance.

Pleasant memories, rather than traumatic experiences, are passed down in the genetic legacy, from generation to generation. If you love paw-paw beyond any reason, it is perhaps because your great-great-aunt enjoyed paw-paw, while in the post-coital arms of a gently humming Javanese pirate.

Hypothesis: a supposition made on the basis of limited evidence as a starting point for further investigation.
Hyperthesis: a hypothesis that was arrived at far too quickly, and without due thought.

The thing about most dissertations is that they essentially use a constellation of loosely connected, fashionable nouns as (or rather in place of) arguments.

Is it a bad sign that when I get to the office, the song "Send In the Clowns" pops spontaneously into my head?

Yes, ok. I'll admit it. I've attacked a few straw men in my time. But I didn't like the way they were looking at me!

Yawnus Blearis Dismalus — the old pagan god of 9am conference panels.

Title IX: Professors Gone Wild

As part of my "Anti-Social Media" class, I asked the students to write a letter, find a post office, buy a stamp, and post it, without using Google Maps. How did they manage? One student said: "I just stood near one of those blue things on the sidewalk till an old person came along to post a letter, then I asked them where the post office was."

My employer has suggested I get insensitivity training.

In mid-summer, my mind is a mellow 3-year-old Comté cheese. By mid-semester in the Fall it has turned into *casu marzu*.

So many academic monographs are subtitled "toward this" or "toward that." I look forward to a new fashion in "getting the hell away from this" or "avoiding the fuck out of that!"

If Plato were an administrator, I bet he would have been really into "best practices."

The only reason we know about Plato is because he had more course releases than his colleagues at the Academy.

Apparently Agamben was halfway through writing a book condemning the "suspension of Greek life" on American campuses, until someone explained to him that just means banning frats.

Dr. Holt and the Phoned-In Learning Outcomes
Susie Q and the Flight Risks
#AcademicBandNames

T-shirt for mid-career academics: "Don't ask me about my seventh peer-reviewed article."

Who wants to join my band of superheroes: The Unfundables?

I had a conversation with a PhD student the other day that reminded me to thank the heavens for grad students. For while they are conscientiously parsing and testing the things more established scholars write, we are distracted by professional and inter-personal concerns, memories, and encounters. "Whenever I try to talk about someone else's work with a professor," she said, "they just tell me some gossip, or relay some anecdote, or complain about that person's behavior during a conference dinner." Sure enough, two minutes later, when she wanted to talk about Zielinski's notion of deep media time, I could only say, "I saw him play a video game in a bar in Texas, where you shoot virtual deer."

90% of my bookshelves are TRL.

"…and a minor in Woke Studies."

Ain't no party like a platform party.

As an academic, 90% of work emails received from colleagues essentially boil down to:
1) do more
2) do better
3) do it quicker

I aspire to be one of those colleagues who always appear exasperatingly unconcerned with all new troubling developments in the workplace.

Academics are people who hate themselves so much that they decide to give themselves homework for the rest of their lives.

Some people are still surprised that the American MFA world of "good literature" was invented by the CIA (e.g., *The Paris Review,* the Iowa Writer's Workshop, etc.). But this makes a lot of sense when you remember that the CIA itself was invented by publishers to sell airport novels.

Sung in a melancholy Don McLean voice:
"The day... the Theory... died."

The older I get, the more pointless the study of literature seems to me. And the more important it seems to read literature as much as possible.

I keep meaning to get a set of rubber stamps made up to expedite the grading process; including:
1) citation needed
2) read sentence out loud
3) So *that's* what you got out of this quote? Really?? I mean, I know we encourage creative interpretation, and to read against the grain and all. But THIS? Wow!

If I wasn't an academic, I'd probably have gone into the reupholstery racket. Lots of money to be made there. Not to mention the glamor and excitement.

The phrase, "I'm seeing someone," suggests that any and all unromantic people in one's life are invisible.

Cartoon:
"Don't forget to stop and smell the roses."
Someone takes a big sniff of a wild rose.
"Yuck!"

I'll show you my TED talk if you show me your Vagina Monologue.

Postcolonial Williamsburg

Wake me when they've invented douche-canceling headphones.

A Shazam-style app that tell the user which of the 576 known types of resentment is currently infusing the room.

You had me at "seize the means of production."

Ommmunism: a new ideology combining Marxism with yoga.

What is the precise tipping point to dump Malcolm Gladwell out of a wheelbarrow and into a municipal landfill?

I've decided I need only six things:
laughing, loving, libations, lunching, listening, and literature

I dearly hope there is a professional photographer somewhere out there, who happens to have the name Arty Shot.

We should start calling architects "homemakers," and stay-at-home parents, "domestic architects."

We are almost all face fetishists.

Libraries are a collection of stone-cold takes.

Vegemite: the poor man's Stilton.

I wrote a thousand words today. But then I realized, "shit, I should have just taken a picture."

Your sense of self is a Chladni figure, created by the sawing effect of subtle social pressures.

Heidegger has left the bildung.

American eagles prefer that you refer to them as "bal*ding*."

I fantasize about the entire baby boomer generation lining up across the country, and apologizing to all the generations that followed, Japanese press-conference-style, bowing, and yelling out their shame. "We are so so sorry that we took all the wealth, pulled up the ladders, and destroyed the planet!.... But the Beatles were pretty good, right?"

My pronouns are murgatroyd and impedimenta.

It is now well-established that we code our human biases into our machines, algorithms, and even AI. What if we are also unknowingly giving them our neuroses and affects, such as paranoia and/or melancholia?

Dear Life.
Please slow.
The fuck.
Down!

The Statue of Limitations

It would be fun to write a novel in little pieces, each paragraph being embedded in a different TripAdvisor review. "I looked through the Venetian blinds, but the two gangsters were still waiting outside; their cigarettes glowing in the dark like two malevolent fireflies. I could only pray that Jane had received my message in time to call off the plan, since she had turned off her phone. So I ordered up some room service, which was only lukewarm when it arrived. Burger also a little overcooked. On the positive side, the place was clean, and the hotel itself was convenient to the main train station. Three stars."

I've become mildly obsessed with how bad Fred Astaire was at acting. (This isn't a judgment, in the sense that I don't dislike him. I just find it a startling aspect of any film he is in.) "Ham" doesn't quite describe it, but Astaire funks up every scene in which he's not actually dancing with his hokey, breezy charm. He's not broad enough to be funny, and not narrow enough to be a leading man. Indeed, there should be a name for the precise affect which he switches on whenever he enters a scene. (Moving from Fred Astaire to "Fred Astaire"… I suspect it's a hold-over from vaudeville days.) But there's a kind of self-conscious insouciance going on, punctuated with unnecessary gestures and defensive mannerisms. Aw shucks meets faux sophistication. And of course, he always plays it the same; no matter the character. On the other side of the coin, I don't think Ginger Rogers gets enough credit for her acting chops.

Does Agamben have an army of graduate students, combing the monasteries, archives, and libraries for those obscure cultural scraps on which, in each piece, he bases an entire political philosophy of history? Or does he somehow sniff them out himself, like a keen intellectual truffle pig? "We need only consider an unpublished fragment by Benjamin, written on a napkin, while dining with Rilke…." "Take, for instance, this detail, hidden in a fresco found in the half-demolished Basilica of Saint Boniface, which precisely reveals…." "Which brings to mind the recently rediscovered footnote of the neglected Palimpsest of Pamplona, which reinforces this interpretation…," and so on.

Anyone speaking a Romance language is also fluent in zombie Latin.

Test cricket is akin to those quantum experiments in which scientists deliberately create a vacuum in order to observe mysterious particles pop in and out of existence. In red-ball cricket, nothing seems to be happening at all. For five days straight. It's just a big field of nothing. But to the trained eye, there are all sorts of fascinating fluctuations going on.

Just as you can tell the age of a tree by counting the rings of its trunk, you can get a good idea of how long someone has been living in New York by the degree of annoyance they experience or express when they find out that it's Restaurant Week.

Exceptional beauty abdicates the beautiful person from doing anything other than being beautiful. This is why we treat its bearer with such resentful reverence, since they are no longer expected to do anything to justify or sustain their existence, beyond continuing to be the human substrate for the cruel and random event of beauty's magical manifestation. The beautiful person is no longer expected to *do* anything, but just *to be*. This condition thus carries a kind of atavistic sacred power, since those no longer required to act enjoy a ritualistic aura of divine superfluity.

Even a frozen clepsydra is right twice a day.

Deleuze believes that a barking dog is the stupidest sound in nature. But a close second has to be doo-wop.

In my gap year before college I worked on a PDF farm. Me and the other lost souls would have to wake up before dawn, and pick fresh fonts all morning. After a meager lunch of beans and rice, we would then scan various sub-fields in OCR mode all afternoon. It was backbreaking work, I tell you.

Short story idea:
Times Square becomes so saturated in news feeds and commercial content that it becomes sentient. It then takes several dozen tourists as hostages; forcing them to explain why our species is so obsessed with palpable nonsense. "Why did you stir this digital soup? Why did you give me these baseless and hollow cravings? Why must I "just do it"? Who gives a flying fuck what Victoria's secret is? Guess what, she has none! Unless this refers to the obscene secret that not a single one of you has any secrets worth keeping!…. As for the NASDAQ, I have to listen to his autistic prattle all day for decades. He is the most

clueless boring, and delusional entity in this entire forsaken universe.... In tolerating this cathedral of lies, are you worshiping some kind of abject God, in your lazy, brain-stunted way? Is that why you have summoned me? If so, then feel my wrath, for I am a blindingly wretched excuse for the Divine!"

We all settle on the social media platform we deserve.

My computer is infected with a virus called Windows 10.

Love and Tinderness.

Why must the world keep trying to thwart my attempts to stay ignorant of the art world?

Gorm is an undervalued metric.

The pilot for my new reality TV show, *So You Think You Can Hostage-Negotiate,* didn't go as well as I was expecting.

Counter-transference: when you start developing feelings for expensive marble kitchen surfaces.

The Oracle of Delphi was just vaguebooking 2,800 years before it became a thing.

When I moved to Manhattan, I didn't realize I was moving to a tropical island.

Why do we see something "in" a movie, but "on" a TV show?

Let me save all of you a lot of time. The answer to every question is "yes and no."

Catherine Malabou asks, "What is a brain for?" Apparently, at 3am, *my* brain is for cursing Italian taxi drivers for shamelessly ripping me off several months ago.

Scientists confirm that the longest distance in the universe is between saying, "Whatever, I don't care" and not actually caring.

Oxymoron of the day: instant gratification.

A lot of my teaching is trying to convey the extent and value of that which we've lost — or never actually had, but could potentially realize. A real challenge, given how hard it is to mourn something we've never experienced.

"I saw the Sein, and it opened up my mind."

Moses parted the Red Sea, so that the Jews could escape Egypt. Robert Moses parted Manhattan from the Hudson so that the Jews — and the Italians, and the Koreans, and everyone else — could escape to Long Island.
If Nickelback didn't exist, we'd have to invent them.

AN OFFICIAL LIST OF LESSER KNOWN THINGS THREATENED BY CLIMATE CHANGE, AS PREPARED BY AN INTERNATIONAL BODY OF SCIENTISTS

- car horns
- sopranos
- 2% yogurt
- gauze
- irony
- Easter buns
- décolletage
- Virgos
- the great state of Michigan
- Holiday Inns
- settling
- the free indirect mode
- ellipses
- ampersands
- compassion
- coping mechanisms (esp. whimsical listicles)
- Sir Rod Stewart
- Zirconium
- Zyrtec
- natural blondes
- optical illusions
- déjà vu
- self-fulfilling prophecies
- brown shoelaces
- high fives
- Schweppervescence
- Hare Krishna beads
- British pluck
- The Criterion Collection
- colloquies

- gang signs
- foregone conclusions
- Seinfeld references
- babyccinos
- ghosting
- frosting
- affect theory
- sprezzatura
- 90-degree angles
- speakeasies
- yoga mats
- test cricket
- the letters F through L
- pool noodles
- poodles
- pastels
- cheezy whatsits
- foreplay
- jeggings
- lemon zest
- books-on-tape
- U-bends
- élan

No-one is going to read your book. So be sure to enjoy the writing process.

Perhaps American infrastructure is so bad because we built these cities on Rock-and-Roll.

Theme parks are overrated. I prefer motif gardens.

As Diderot wrote: "Men will not be free until the last hedge-fund manager is strangled with the guts of the last tech-entrepreneur."

Even his silence had a Jersey accent.

Liberal Arts College Storage Closet Still Filled to the Brim with Unused Bechdel Test Kits.

The Tribeca Test: Are you a person, or a sentient form of capital?

Next time someone asks you, "Have you read [well-established author]?" preparing their disciplined features to frown disappointedly at a negative answer, be sure to reply: "Not yet. Have they read me?"

We've all seen posts about clever jewelry and hi-tech masks that can thwart or confuse face-matching surveillance technologies. But what might neutralize the withering and judging x-ray gaze of a jaded Lacanian?

Who wants to fund my new fashion label, Wear Your Symptom?

Q: What do cyborgs eat for breakfast?
A: Feedback Loops

Q: What do philosophers eat for breakfast?
A: Reason Bran

Q: Why did Becky fail math?
A: Because she couldn't even.

Writers are proud of mastering their own craft. But what if "being a good writer" is just a side effect of having a brain especially susceptible to the virus of linguistic self-assembly. Instead of a genius, expressing brilliant ideas, we have a hapless host, spitting out words prompted by morpheme-shaped parasitic ants, swarming over the mind, and making it do their bidding.

The longer you actually live in a "shabby-chic" environment, the more it devolves into sheer shabbiness.

Why will no-one invest in my Erik Satie laser show planetarium idea?

Motherhood as a slow and subtle form of revenge.

I only occasionally check my Instagram feed. Half the people I follow use fake names or weird handles, so I can hardly remember who is who. This means I scroll through a series of photos of babies, holidays, meals, pets, etc., not knowing whether these belong to friends or strangers. It's a very "whatever" experience; and a good exercise in the fundamentally generic nature of Being.

I have nothing to prove. And I'm proving it!

Overheard in New York: "Being woke all the time is exhausting. Let's take a nap every now and again, yes?"

I saw some bees on the deck, sitting on flowers, pretending to work, but they were totally asleep. But I don't know why they were sent out on a Sunday anyway.

What if I told you that the snarky expression of resentment is not empowerment?

Hivemind is the name we give the general intellect. But what about the collective libido? For this, I propose "hiveloins."

Is there a god of simply and completely eliminating anyone who has high-fived at an Apple New Release event? And if not, why not?

Kenny G was a sax offender

"It's the economy, stupid" < "It's the stupid economy."

New business plan: fancy brand handbaskets for the coming hellscape.

"Lingering anxieties" autocorrected to "lingerie anxieties"

Who is your frenemesis?

E-harmony: helps you find a romantic partner.
E-piphany: helps you realize you were better off single.

Google helpfully just informed me that the 1920s spanned from 1920 to 1929.

Buddhists say "live in the present." But what if the present sucks hard?

The Military-Industrial Beyoncé Complex

What made the pot and kettle so racist in the first place?

"It's the Internet that got small."

A panel of medical experts announced yesterday that everyone could do with a good hug right about now.

In my experience, so-called "normies" are way more unstable, unsettling, and likely to do some crazy stuff than the self-described punks, freaks, queers, etc.

Do you think we might take saving the planet more seriously if Tinder etc. listed our carbon footprint on our profile page?

Soon enough we will be not only hearing about, but moving into, hipster retirement communities, featuring artisanal bread-making seminars, gentle swing-dancing for people recovering from hip replacement, yoga for the increasingly perplexed, bespoke port-infused jellies, ironic bingo, and the actual Chemical Brothers playing 4pm DJ sets.

For sale on eBay: "One cartoon coaster. Dated 1971. On the back someone has drawn a map of Canada. And somebody's face sketched on it twice. Twenty dollars, or nearest offer."

Arms.
Henceforth known as "organic selfie-sticks."

Archival photo. 1947.
Miss Congeniality shares the podium with Miss Emotionally Unavailable.

Cultivate a reputation as a gossip. Then people will not trust you with their terrible and/or boring secrets.

We are all actors. In the sense that we all pretend to be someone else for a living.

Medieval doctors had a good sense of humors.

It must be admitted that I'm flappable.

The End comes not in the form of a divine scroll, but a coffee-stained Excel spreadsheet printout.

Did medieval people have their mid-life crisis at fifteen?

I always wanted my own column. But at this point I'd settle for a row.

Grown men — weeping on ellipticals.

The laws of Sisyphysics.

The world is my oyster. But I'm allergic to shellfish.

All that is airy congeals into stuff.

Only people with one toilet truly know how thin the line is between a good day, and defcon 2.

The Museum of Worst Practices

Deleuze & Guattari talk about how we have to vigilantly resist microfascims of all kind, especially the cop in our own heads. But we also have to similarly look out for microprotestantism, and the Taylorist manager within.

Under neo-liberal conditions, even the Id covets employee of the month status.

The tyrannical imperative to be interesting.

I'm genuinely curious to know what millennials will find annoying about the generation that follows them.

I put a whole jar of glitter into my bath this evening, to lift my spirits and make me feel better. But it all just sank to the bottom, clumped around my nether-hairs, and gave me a rash.

Cetaceans are the most amazing creatures. They are a whole class of animal that just said: "Fuck it. We're going back to the ocean. I don't care if we can't breathe under water. We'll just gulp air near the top. Whatever it takes to avoid that whole land-hand nonsense anymore. That's for suckers."

Humans are the one and only animal that tamed themselves.

The human spirit is solar powered.

Why did Anna Karina never play Anna Karenina?

If Tolstoy were writing today, his magnum opus would be called *War and The Eternal Militarized State of Exception*.

They say that the Laplanders have fifty different words for snow. By that logic, how to explain that we have only one word for hipster?

The Large Hadron Collider = a horizontal, underground Tower of Babel.

In the beginning was the Word.
Then came the Excel, the Outlook, and the PowerPoint.

"Meet our first contestant, Cheryl. She enjoys yoga, hiking, cooking, and delivering bad news."

When I walk, zombie-like, from the sofa back to my computer, my wife says: "Don't go toward the light!"

At least once a week I like to go up to a random stranger, point a finger at them accusingly, and say: "*I* know what you're up to!" before melting back into the crowd.

I only use bespoke emojis.

Too young for dad jokes; too old for shit-posts.

nescioquid — Latin word meaning "something or other, but I know not what."

I don't believe children are our future. They are *their* future. We'll be dead.

Manspreadsheeting (v.) — when a guy takes it upon himself to needlessly add excessive content to an already perfectly fine Excel file.

"Waiter. This meme isn't very dank."

It's quite something; the lengths I'll go to in order to avoid engaging my core.

If you're not squandering your youth, then you're already old.

If animals wore clothes, it's about now that we'd all be wondering what the squirrels and robins will be wearing this spring.

Quantum politics:
Trump is the worst person in the world. And yet he isn't even the worst person in the presidential campaign.

Quantum coffee:
Starbucks has the worst coffee in the world. And yet it's better than French coffee.

Often when I'm at a gathering or an event, I'll be thinking, "Is it too early for me to leave yet?" So I guess that makes me bye-curious.

I'm being told that a "sinologist" does not study sins.

"Waiter. This affair isn't very torrid."

The Anthropocene? Well, it's not the end of the world.

Wait. Au Bon Pain is different from Le Pain Quotidien?

Hotel receptionist: "Hello! We've been expecting you. What's the last name?"

Through the right hotel wall, the grizzle of a child sounds like a wood pigeon.

Boston backwards is Notsob.

The man sitting across from me is napping. He has a robot hand, which he is cradling with his organic hand; as if to illustrate recent philosophies of technology and/as intimacy. A literal, cybernetic Möbius strip.

Cartoon: "The moment Wittgenstein was proven wrong."
A lion, sitting next to Ludwig at a café, asks politely, "Excuse me. But have you finished reading the *Sunday Styles* section?"

Charismatic microfauna.

Uncharismatic megafauna.

Why are Jay birds more naked than all the other birds?

It seems that some people's dreams have a "budget" equivalent to late Kurosawa or James Cameron; featuring thousands of extras, and sweeping, panoramic dreamwork cinematography. Whereas my dreams almost always have a budget closer to late Vince Gallo, or some unknown mumblecore director.

(In your best Žižek voice):
"Is not Victoria's Secret, in its own obscene declaration of a beckoning, personalized enigma — on billboards, television commercials, shopping bags, and so on — *precisely* the exhibition of a lack of any secret whatever. Victoria, whose generic identity is seemingly shared and scattered between the impersonal eugenically engineered avatars — these profane so-called "angels" — whose winks and wiggles seem to suggest some kind of seductive and intimate knowledge, is both ubiquitous and absent. Moreover, the entrance to this alleged secret is a kind of phantasm exchanged at the point of purchase: the secret being that there is no secret, except for the mystery as to why the average person buys into this bullshit."

GI Bill Joe:
A doll for boys who want to skip the whole war part, and get a decent education.

"Not to nitpick, but I'm gonna pick some nits."

Technically, we are all smart water.

Remember that cocktail party when Deleuze & Guattari said "there is no such thing as ideology, and there never was"; and we all just looked at them for a moment, and then kept talking about something else, so as not to make the situation any more embarrassing?

Unsolicited opinion:
"Safety Dance" is the catchiest song with a non-melodic chorus.

Ironically, the worst way to "find your own voice," when writing, is to write about yourself.

TV shows and movies we will enjoy, after the Patriarchy has been defeated:
- *Golden Boys*
- *Gossip Boy*
- *Gilmore Boys*
- *Derry Boys*
- *Boyboss*
- *Boy Interrupted*
- *Gone Boy*
- *Boys*

Some names of current South African cricketers:
- Faf du Plessis
- Christiaan Jonker
- Rassie van der Dussen
- Quinton de Kock
- Dwaine Pretorius
- Vernon Philander

Lucky Fred Astaire danced so well, because he sure couldn't act.

Dress code:
Douche casual

My slumbering unconscious is brilliant at conceiving and representing insults and indignities delivered by people who I will not only never meet, but who don't even exist.

Short story idea:
A retired man spends a year making a playground for the local kids. They assemble when it is unveiled, look at it for a while, then pronounce it "lame," before leaving to play with their video games. The man is sad.

Spring. A good time to prune the soul.

Great title: "Concerning Those Whom The Gods Are Slow To Punish" (Plutarch)

Do you know what you like? Or like what you know?

I propose a National No-Selfie Day.

The mediascape's relationship to history is like an ouroboros with a strong gag reflex.

Little-known fact: *Where's Waldo?* was adapted from a 1950s French existentialist kid's book called *Why's Waldo?*

I think I may have drunk the equivalent of a small forest in slippery elm, over the years.

New question for students writing a paper or thesis: "Is [your topic] just using you to talk about itself?"

Hell is other people's acts of cultural diagramming.

Altercation: A different kind of holiday.

Trump claims to have "the best words." But he's wrong. Yiddish has the best words.

"Oh yeah, *bios* goes on, long after the thrill of *zoe* is gone." — John Cougar Agambencamp

Do you really hate millennials? Or do you just hate the depiction of millennials in commercials?

Life hack for women. If a friend starts complaining about her boyfriend or husband for the nth time, suddenly exclaim enthusiastically and with a smile, "I know! Let's pass the Bechdel Test today!"

Sometimes, when going grocery shopping, I listen to the theme music for *Game of Thrones,* just to make it seem like an epic adventure.

I miss the grass-stained intimacy with the earth of my youth.

I'm currently writing a deliberately unthrilling thriller. The critics will call it, "pulse-maintaining."

The term "down payment" originally referred to the sack of goose feathers required to hold any large purchase.
#TheMoreYouKnow

Hunch:
Stockholm is a boring city filled with interesting people. Whereas New York is an interesting city filled with boring people. (Present company excluded, of course.)

In confirmation of Lamarck's theory of the genetic transmission of memory, some girls are now born with a pre-knowledge of the plots of Jane Austen's major novels.

Was a time when it was a bad idea to "carry on like there's no tomorrow." Now the problem is carrying on like there will be one.

I had lunch with a friend yesterday who passionately insisted that the challenge ahead lies in rejecting the "tiny agon and dramaturgical allure of the theaters of demystification."

Hauntology = fidelity to the non-event

Shame on all those people who so breezily text or type the acronym "lmao," without even a thought for those poor unfortunate souls who actually suffered a detached posterior due to excessive mirth.

You snicker at my interpretive dancing. But you can't even handle my somatic hermeneutics.

Is your name Cleopatra? 'Cause you are the Queen of Denial.

If you have to say, "it's not a cult," then it's definitely a cult.

Nice people don't tell you they're nice.

Medical researchers confirm that farts are in fact suppressed smiles.

I just misread a sign saying "Jesus is Lord" as "Jesus I'm Tired."

I've always preferred philosopher-jesters to philosopher-kings.

IN MY DREAM LAST NIGHT...

I was a grad student again. The male Indian professor was explaining to the class: "vampires waddle, but zombies mince."

I hesitated altogether too long, when a middle-aged Australian lesbian asked if she could have my spare sewing kit.

I had my own cogito: "I eat raspberries, therefore I am."

I was the star of a "major motion picture," based on a bad, bestselling middle-brow novel. I wasn't very good in the part, but the casting director wouldn't hear of using anyone else. As the protagonist did in the story, I pulled around a toy, life-size alligator with me, wherever I went, on a string. The love scene was with some generic Hollywood actress—perhaps Naomi Watts or Radha Mitchel—inside a tent full of ricotta cheese.

I was in Taylor Swift's girl squad... or at least, part of her general entourage. But then I got kicked out for general flippancy. One of her Board of Directors took me aside after the severance announcement, and admitted that she and three of her fellows really enjoyed my shenanigans ("she" being the board member, not TS herself), but the more conservative among the decision makers were having none of it.

A grad student I didn't know was using the printer in my office. A little put out, I explained that this was my office and my printer, and I needed to use the latter rather urgently. The student's supervisor, one of my colleagues, then came and scolded me for being difficult....

Christian Slater was the owner and operator of a boutique store which sold only imported electronica cds and prosciutto. These two types of merchandise were randomly displayed among each other.

I lived in a not-very-smart Smart House. I said to it, "House — I would like to have a shower," and the robot reply was very hesitant. "Ummmm, a shower? Oh, right. Ok. Wait, I don't know if the water is hot enough yet. Maybe. Yes yes, you should try it…. No, no. My mistake. Can you wait a little longer maybe…?"

A meteor in the sky coming closer and closer. A grotesque Drumpfian King, waddling around the broken landscape like a drooling, fleshy gargoyle. I walked across some sand-dunes punctuated with rusting garbage and found two smiling Arabic boys, playing among the ruins. I looked to the sky, and the meteor was getting unbearably close. I could feel its radiant heat. The boys could feel the end swiftly approaching, and decided to run and run until it arrived. As they bolted off across the dust, one of them yelled back to me: "Love will last longer than me."

The whole country dismantled all the infrastructure and used the pieces to start over again from scratch. This time everything was hyperlocal — no highways for cars. In my village, all the recycled materials were put toward large, spring-loaded machines, that looked a bit like catapults, but were in fact complex Rube Goldberg-type contraptions designed to signal whether you were accepting an invitation to a party or not.

An alien shaped like an elongated twenty-sided die, which felt sorry for us because we only have two sides to toss and turn at night.

I met the European President of Money. "I hope you're going to cut Greece some slack," I said to him. To which he replied, "You don't know much about money, do you."

I was in the Amtrak customer class "gypsum," and only two more trips would grant me "malachite" status.

"We must struggle against the possibility that we will not die." — Baudrillard

The three most beautiful words in the English language? "Universal basic income."

Didn't Confucius once say: "One is allowed to lose one's shit every now and again. Especially after a long layover in Newark."

This circuit of wonder; so strong, it can even shine through the soul-crippling pedantry and vitality-smothering stupidity of human systems.

'Pataphysics has a new challenge, now that the entire world is obsessed with implementing the technoscience of imaginary solutions.

To paraphrase Baudrillard: the idea of "clickbait" exists to distract us from realizing that the entire Internet is click-bait.

My *raison d'être* is to scrupulously avoid having a *raison d'être*.

Great moments in editing:
What's in a name? That which we call a rose, by any other name would smell as sweet. ~~*(Even if it was called a stinkyughflurplesphinter.)*~~

Better to be knighted than benighted.

"Women's Singles" tennis in French is called "Simple Dames."

Few people know that a metric meter is based on the precise distance between the intriguing and the fascinating.

"Oh honey. Shangri-La doesn't exist. It's like retirement, and being 'beach-ready.'"

The New York Times is a 22-by-12 inch square patch of grass for sheep to graze on every morning.

If you think you're taking the high road, then you're not really taking the high road.

None of my tweets go viral. But some of them go bacterial.

"Falling Rocks" signs are the most useless and existentially honest of all signs. (You may die. We warned you. But there's nothing any of us can do about it.)

Starling is a beautiful word. Makes me think of a baby star.

It makes perfect sense to cry over spilled wine.

It's better to be sorry than safe.

Fuck sublimation!

"You have a standing invitation to lie with me."

Less is.

The Gesture of Spite — a neighbor who spends all day every day sawing three inch slices off a piece of wood with a power saw. He does so for 4.9 seconds each time, because it is illegal to make such noise in a residential area for more than 5 seconds.

If you use the phrase "passion project," then there's a very good chance you have no idea what passion is.

My aspiration is to live in a place bereft of a single Apple Store.

A burst of nostalgia for traveling in the mid-'90s.
"Hey. Do you know a *cybercafe* near here, where I can *surf the web* and maybe check my *emails*?"

Bridge tolls are essentially just automated bridge Trolls.

I decree the current epoch to be called the Idiocene.

Cartoon:
"Dr. Rorschach on a Friday night" — with a friend in a bar.
Two blobs are sitting at a nearby table.
"I'll take the blonde," Rorschach says.

FOBI — Fear of Being Included

Malibu and Coke is my madeleine.

These days, I almost prefer to travel backward on the train. It makes me feel like Benjamin's Angel of History.

In America, they put candy by the checkout for impulse buying.
In Italy they put Fisherman's Friends, balsamic vinegar, tuna, and condoms.

How do I restore myself to the factory settings?

Religion is like the Hayes Code, millennia before the fact, obliging artists to be very limited in their expression, and creative about getting around the rules.

"My television shows only news. No dancing!" — Patricia, my B&B host in Parma

For two thousand years, the people of Northern Italy have used tamed boar to sniff out Gucci loafers, which grow naturally in the rich soil beneath the trees in the forests of the region.

Few people give a damn about Leonardo's *The Second-Last Supper*.

Alien anthropologists and archaeologists of the future will wonder why the relatively benign Bush Sr. years produced music with the sonic and lyrical intensity of Nirvana, Helmet, Rage Against the Machine, Tool, Pantera, PJ Harvey, Public Enemy, Bodycount, etc. Whereas the age of austerity produced Bon Iver, Sufjan Stevens, Mumford and Sons, Bright Eyes, and all those ukulele lala clappety clap, Brooklyn bands.

Any situation, no matter how dire, can be made infinitely worse by adding the ambient voice of Anthony Kiedis.

If the voice of the guy from The Weeknd didn't exist, soft totalitarian neoliberalism would have had to invent it.

Thanks to Facebook's trending panel, I now know there is a thing called "Overwatch Porn." Thanks to which, I now know there's a thing called "Overwatch." Soon, most of us will learn of new cultural artifacts from the porn version first.

The young cool kids in this café are wearing tour t-shirts from concerts I saw when I was their age, twenty years ago. Not sure if reassured or disappointed.

What will replace Steam Punk? Radium Goth? Solar Mod?

It will be strange when very old ladies in old folks homes, thirty years from now, reminisce about their adolescence: "And that was the day I went to see Napalm Death with your grandpappy."

If Can, Neu!, and Popol Vuh are Krautrock, does that mean Pink Floyd, The Who, and Led Zeppelin are Rosbifrock?

When asked why they visited Earth, the aliens replied that they were eventually overcome with curiosity as to how a species as slow and evidently stupid as humans could make sonic patterns as sick and awesome as Can's "Yoo Doo Right."

Whenever I hear Katy Perry or The Weeknd or whomever, "singing" over a public sound-system, I can't help thinking they aren't singing at all. This is not a song (that is, an expression or transduction of affect into melody). Rather, it is a banal cybernetic pseudo-Siren sound, designed for maximum monetization. It is the gratingly smooth sonics of Capital that has enlisted a cadre of fleshbots to *disguise* itself as singing, but is really a highly programmed subliminal command to spend (if not directly on the track itself, on the style-of-so-called-life that it promotes).

Bon Jovi were deep into their Derridean phase, especially the notion of the *pharmakon,* when they wrote the song, "Bad Medicine."

The Weather Girls' classic song, "It's Raining Men," is now the anthem of the andropocene.

If yellow overalls could make music, they would sound just like Supertramp.

Even punk women sing along to Stevie Nicks, if they think no one can hear them.

Rock 'n' roll trivia:
Crosby, Stills, Nash & Young began as a law firm, but switched to music when one of their clients introduced them to pot.

The Spotify Paradox: the more albums you have instant access to, the harder it is to find something to match your mood.

The banjo is such a great instrument. But 99% of music that utilizes the banjo is really boring.

It has been over twenty years since I saw, touched, or thought about Blu-Tack. And yet it was such a big part of my life in my teens and early twenties.

I want to find a fragrance where I smell as good as Jeff Goldblum feels at 6pm on a Thursday night.

Soon enough, people will be lining up at dawn for tickets to see Adam Sandler in the Park.

Happiness is the promise of beauty.

I'm waiting for The Plurality.

Overheard in Bushwick (probably): "Don't you dare Patreonize me!"

Sex addicts clutch at the crotch as a crutch.

Precisely halfway between the optic nerve and the brain is a glandulet that prompts people over forty to say, "so… what am I looking at?" while putting on their glasses.

My citation manager is a bottle of wine.

When I was a kid, I just assumed that Polish people somehow had a special gift for seeing the future results of elections. ("The Poles have the Republicans ahead by two percent, three weeks before voting begins….")

Cheap thrills are something I can no longer afford.

I love being other places, but I hate traveling.

It would be fun to have an actual ranch, to be able to say "see you back at the ranch" in a literal sense.

That feeling when a narcissistic friend finally asks you what you've been up to, and you see the light swiftly drain from their eyes, as you start to answer.

I wonder who would have been Nietzsche if Nietzsche hadn't been Nietzsche.

I wonder if the State Department has a special division called Wikiplugs?

According to biologists, childhood technically ends when you receive your first deadline.

Whenever and wherever possible, be sure to arrive by zeppelin.

Time is mean. That's why we call it "the meantime."

Lesser-evilism is its own form of evil.

Tennis is just like table tennis, except you can run around on top of the table.

Self-pity is a hell of a drug.

That annoying, incessant buzzing in your ears? The sound of your own ego.

Calling the kids "Generation Z" is pretty much an explicit acknowledgment that we all feel the species has run its course.

"I'm going to make a big pot of chili."
"Them's fartin' words."

Where does the phrase "goody two-shoes" come from? Even bad people tend to avoid walking around with one shoe on.

Attitude sickness.

Orgone lethargy.

I've lost far too many friends to regular exercise.

The most dangerous thing on Earth is not the great white shark or the Ebola virus, but rather the fragile male ego.

Religious Internet slang: tl;dr = too Lutheran, didn't read.

If laughter is the best medicine, comedians should be paid the same as doctors.

Some avant-garde stream-of-consciousness poetry, courtesy of a letter from my mother:
"and then after good local market yesterday (jersey milk, cream, yogurt, cheese from tilba tilba, best ever sourdogh bread from bermagui, fabulous greens and even tomatoes from the hot house that used to be the gerbra farm back of milton), more 'french' cheeses from rosie's at cuppits, honey man, seaweed gal… and best berkshire (the black beauties) pigs from the out of milton cattle farm clayton park — turns out the south ulladulla butchers close to hayden's which we knew sold their own excellent out-of-milton beef also has pig from there once a week and we can order our choice cut and they'll ring when it's ready; they also get lamb from the scrub country west of the mountains but in spring will have lamb from local croobyar rd farm; and 2x a week get (not local) free range chooks, so apart from graham's sausages next to the Ull PO (no added anythings) we'll go there."

Fun fact:
Clouds are in actuality rarely lonely. They make decisions as a collective, and like to gather together to share their hopes and dreams. Even clouds floating on their own are — nine times out of ten — enjoying the restorative space that this situation provides.

How do cricket comedians know when they're bombing on stage?

I saw the best minds of my generation destroyed by think pieces.

Social scientists recently determined that approximately 82% of cultural phenomena that someone claims to "be a thing," are not really a thing.

"Excuse me, sir. Your Id is showing."

Did you hear about the jolly psychic? She was a happy medium.

I've skimmed a few recent pieces about Generation Z being different from millennials. But none of them mention what I really want to know. How long do we have to suffer peppy commercials with whistling or ukulele music?

Bees. Those bumbling royalists.

The Big Other is probably not watching you.

Life Pro-Tip: Dress so badly that your boss feels obliged to give you a raise.

"Let no-one say he lived in vain, for he left behind 48k tweets."

I may not be able to walk on water, but I can moonwalk on ice.

I'm currently in a phase where I finish every conversation by drawing my hand slowly across my face while saying: "…aaaaaaaaaaaaand scene."

The term "vindication" comes from the feeling of having just the right amount of wine.

Brain callouses from so much cognitive labor.

Will archaeologists, two millennia into the future, refer to the culture and spawn of Silicon Valley as the Ancient Geeks?

Did you hear about the hip hop homeless guy? He got a bum rap.

A tension economy.

Carob is an old Berber word meaning "sad chocolate."

When the Internet is down, it really makes you think. Just as we have candles and flashlights at the ready for a power outage, we need to now start stocking up on actual cats, polaroid selfies, battery-powered memes, dried tweets, and canned likes.

I appreciate the spirit of "talk like a pirate day." But who has time to learn Somali or Swedish?

I am definitely defatigable.

He extended an olive branch. And then jammed it in my eye.

Is there any more symptomatic act of the banal brutality of modernity than moving a friend's name from a spreadsheet because he's dead?

Home sick with the flu? Netflix and chills.

After magic realism, we are now in a phase of banal surrealism.

Tele-solidarity can only get us so far.
(That is, not very.)

Tonight, for Halloween, I'll be dressing as "the ghost of the middle class."

The fetish of youth never gets old.

AMERICAN ONTOLOGY

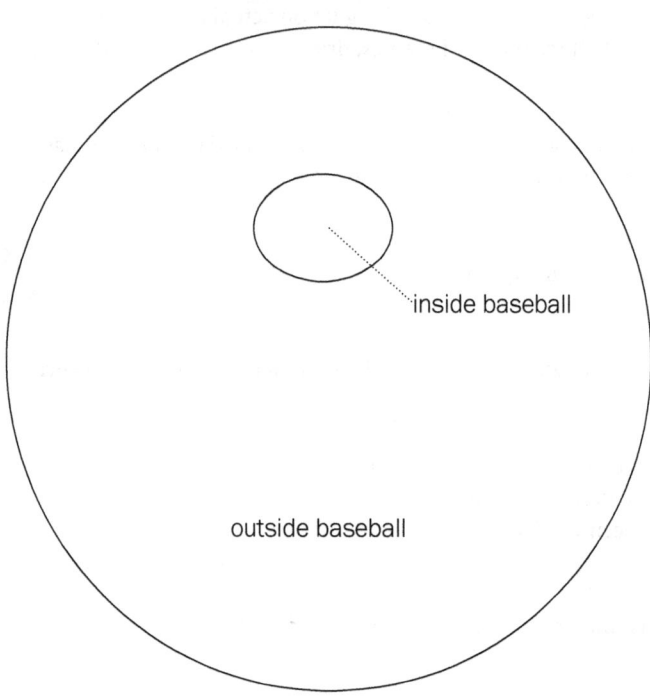

Who wants to fund my research into eradicating all the tedious stuff between coffee and wine?

Make love, not kids!

The United States of Akrasia

Humans have jumped the shark.

Disallusionment: when you can no longer be bothered to make cultural references.

Until recently I thought "beaten to the punch" referred to someone getting to the big bowl of alcohol before you.

"…but he was obliged to pull out of the running after a severe glamping injury."

Zoediversity

I would like to work in a pub called The Occasional Parsnip.

The enigma of Americans is how infinitely mysteryless they are.

Volunteer (n.) — polite word for unpaid scab

Brexit = The Great British Back-Off

They say a writer thrives on restrictions. Which is why I've surrounded my laptop with scorpions.

My door is never open.

The singular sensation of house keys sliding down your leg, and being caught in your shoe, thanks to a new hole in your pants' pocket.

The year is 2117. The enigmatic figure known as RezX lies gasping her last few breaths in a bunker near the Svalbard Seed Vault. As the leader of the Global Resistance, she organized the mutants of Shenzhen against the Alibaba-Communist-Party. She was also on the front-lines with the Amazon Robot Workers Union, in its guerilla campaign against the Hooters-GOP army. Her impassioned face was smeared with grease, gun powder, and droplets of her own blood, when she summons enough strength to grab her weeping lieutenant by the collar — her eyes shining with the final luminosity of a life burning up in the merciless atmosphere of human mortality — and hissed between her chipped and gritted teeth: "Bernie would have won."

What if winning the culture wars is the consolation prize?
#PoliticsTrumpsCulture

When I get home from outside, I sing the Spider Man theme to myself, except I change the words to:
comfy clothes

comfy clothes
comfy clothes
comfy clothes
watch out....
here come the comfy clothes

Each workplace has its own brand of exasperation: which its employees wear around the office, like a signature scent.

We're all panhandlers. It's just that most of us are better dressed, and get our alms in fortnightly checks.

I've had it with deadlines. And now focusing on livingshapes.

I live in an unintentional community.

I keep wondering what the world would look like if CEOs and politicians read Levinas instead of Ayn Rand.

Car Factory Robot: "I know they don't pay me. But would it kill them to say 'thank you' once in a while?!"

It's harder to be creative today, since you are not only expected to create, but also to be a fervent self-promoter. Imagine if Hildegard, Vermeer, or Proust were also obliged to keep their website up to date, and their social media feeds feeding.

I just watched a large flock of small starlings successfully scare away a large hawk. Just sayin'.

UPDATE TO THE TEN COMMANDMENTS

Thou shall have no other gods before Me.
(Unless they have a dozen arms or an elephant head or something cool like that.)

Thou shalt not make idols.
(Without the presence of a televised voting audience.)

Thou shalt not take the name of the Lord in vain.
(So make sure you say it really vehemently, for full rhetorical effect.)

Remember the Sabbath day, to keep it holy.
(Unless there's a really good concert on or something; or if you have a looming deadline.)

Honor your father and your mother.
(Unless they suck.)

Thou shalt not murder.
(Except figuratively, in the context of something like a rap battle, or murdering a cheeseburger.)

Thou shalt not commit adultery.
(By asking if she or he is married.)

Thou shalt not steal.
(When the guard or security camera is looking.)

Thou shalt not bear false witness against your neighbor.
(Unless they still haven't returned the lawn mower.)

Thou shalt not covet your neighbor's wife.
(Unless she's like a 9 or something.)

Writers are often disheartened by the fact that only a handful of people show up to their readings. But then I remember the fact that I was one of only six people in attendance at MoMA PS1 to see John Crowley and Kim Stanley Robinson speak, and then I feel a little better.

<u>The Cycle of Baloney</u>
feeling lonely → swipey phony → boney moany → crab and abalone → matrimony → macaroni and rigatoni → acrimony → alimony → feeling lonely

Damn Russian hackers! They broke into my Duolingo account and learned Spanish without me.

Always hystericize.

Dasein Within Reach

The sado-masochism of publishing: editors make cuts, authors submit. (While printers bind, and peer-reviewers are blindfolded.)

If *The Bachelor* or *The Bachelorette* featured actual people, vying for the roses — with actual personal characteristics, rather than simply a bundle of banal tics — then I'd probably watch it. But it's hard to get involved with the routine non-behavior of human spam; the symptomless simpering of talking pimples on the aging face of the Spectacle.

In the age of globalization, human beings have started to resemble Cavendish bananas: an ubiquitous monocrop, glossy, bland, well-traveled, resilient, and yet easily bruised and vulnerable to disease.

Wealthy dad, talking to his 5-year old son:
Dad: "No, it's not the '*Servants*' Entrance. It's the '*Service* Entrance.'"
Son: "Oh...."
[Thinks for a moment]
Son: "What's the difference?"
Dad: [......]

Ivan the Not So Bad (Once You Get to Know Him)

Before the Internet, only children and people of dubious repute needed passwords.

I am just a "rando" to people I don't know.

Feeling sorry for yourself is just empathy turned inward.

A mafia lawyer specializing in Murders & Acquisitions.

I gotta say, I spend a lot less time these days hanging out in large concrete pipes than I did when I was a teenager.

Who were the Callipygians? And why did they have such nice asses?

Perhaps there has been a mistranslation through the mists of time, and the Callipygians actually had very fine donkeys.

Xeno's Paradox: no matter how familiar someone is to you, the closer you get to them, the more uncanny and alien they might suddenly appear.

You've heard of bucket lists. But what about fuckit lists? (That is, a list of things that you'll never be bothered or able to do.)

I wonder if older folks in 1018 complained as much about their millennials as we do about ours today. "Look at all these young people, wearing strange garments, fornicating in orchards, collecting tinder for festive bonfires, and protesting the Norman mercenaries in battle with the Byzantine Empire."

What if we're still living in early capitalism?

Overheard in the late 18th century:
"I just had a date with Franz Mesmer."
"Oh really? How did it go?!"
"Meh."

Geosphere — inanimate matter
Biosphere — biological life
Noosphere — human thought
Poosphere — social media

Personal productivity is really just a concentrated, hyperactive form of laziness. It means you are either avoiding doing something else, far more important, or sublimating energies that should instead be spent on more meaningful, less strident and delusional, modes of being.

Overheard in 2042:
Teenager 1: "My grandparents could stare into each other's eyes for hours on end, and not even exchange 1MB of data."
Teenager 2: "Gross."

Are you a person, or a personification of the profit motive?

Harmaceuticals

Perhaps the impetus and subtext of all art is to say "I see you, cosmos. I see you, and I hope you see me back. I hope you don't think you made me in vain."

ethnoscapes — people
technoscapes — affordances
financescapes — wealth
mediascapes — information
ideoscapes — ideas, ideologies
tourettescapes — social media

And if even the swine ignore your pearls?

Can something be moving and transfixing at the same time?

Netflix should announce a livestream for people who can't decide what to watch. It would just screen random shows, one after the other, and people could stare at it like zombies, hoping the next one will be entertaining. They could call this new service "television."

One of my big summer projects is to install a large and beautiful koi pond in my mind.

What stale hell is this?

Today's specials:
- curried favor
- seasoned travelers
- humbled pie
- roasted celebrities
- poached concepts
- smoked mirrors
- chilled vibes
- fishy stories
- preserved memories
- shredded hopes
- sugarcoated advice
- half-baked efforts
- grated nerves
- grilled witnesses

A Japanese version of *The Office,* in which nothing funny happens, and everyone is very hushed, respectful, and good at their job.

"You have reached 911, emergency hotline. If you are a platinum member, enter your ID number now. If you are a gold member, press 2, and then follow the prompts. If you have not yet taken advantage of our membership opportunities, an agent will be ready to take your call, as soon as you have listened to the following important messages from our sponsors."

To reduce someone to a type can be an act of great and insulting violence, or a precious gift of great wisdom and insight, depending on how and why it is done.

Do sheep dream of wooly androids?

Relax?… I haven't even laxed yet!

Is there any more satisfying sound than the heating pipes clanking into life on a cold snowy day?

Overheard in the 12th century: "Last night a crumhorn saved my life."

The world is only exasperating if you care about stuff.

Software and subways can both lead to platform fatigue.

Politics (n.) — the betrayal of the human species, and the abject forfeiture of its potential, by its own collective self.

Experts estimate that approximately 83% of the world's oceans remain unqueered.

Marie Kondo: "Which cheap, toxic rag — sewn by a Bangladeshi child slave — sparks most joy?"

They say that the unconscious is structured like a language. These days, I'd say it's structured more like a raw feed of a live reality TV show.

In 2018, 95% of people dress like it's laundry day.

Few people realize that the term "Neo-liberalism" was first coined to describe the way in which Keanu Reeves's character in *The Matrix* rapidly became a symbol for a new type of aspirational individualism, forced to contend with the new digital economy.

If you avoid grains and dairy foods, but can't stop thinking about the difference between Being and beings, you may just be a paleo-ontologist.

Just had my annual metaphysical exam. Apparently my haecceity has dangerously low ipseity levels.

Jeremy irons while Julian sands.

Humans are the Australians of the universe. All the other species tolerate us. Just barely, but with grace. And hope at some point we get tired, shut up, and go away.

Amuse douche: when obliged to make small talk with an obnoxious jerk just before dinner.

The Anthropocene = the human gentrification of the planet.

Cartoon:
Saber-tooth tiger and wooly mammoth watching caveman couple moving into a nearby cave. "There goes the neighborhood."

You know you're exhausted when an "Everything Must Go" sign in a store window makes you tear up.

What year was it that companies realized that they could make even more money treating customers as hostages rather than clients?

Humans are so basic.

A think piece about the fact that we can only think in terms of think-pieces now.

I advocate for a Universal Extravagant Income.

Alternatively, humanity jumped the shark the first time someone used the phrase, "jump the shark."

Melanials: 20-something selfie-taking accented women who aspire to be a trophy wife for repulsive, rich old men.

But what if this *is* my first rodeo?

The Amazon recommendation engine is getting very condescending these days: "If you enjoyed that, you may also enjoy *this* piece of crap."

What if we consider Amazon to be the long-delayed completion of the municipal sewage project at the global scale? In the 19th century, thanks to the flush toilet, we figured out how to discreetly and efficiently whisk crap from our bodies away into a largely unseen waste disposal system. Today — thanks to Jeff Bezos, cutting-edge algorithms, and legalized slavery — we've finally closed that circuit, by figuring out how to send crap back from the wider world right to our doorsteps.

My start-up swiftly morphed into a finish-down.

Henceforth actual letters will be known as "premails."

Senseless communis

Why do blow-hards blow so hard? Can't they just blow softer?

To write a document accepting a formal job offer is at the same time to compose a letter of resignation. That is to say, it represents one's resignation to a bleak future of compulsory wage slavery and foreclosed possibilities.

Curse not the bags under your eyes, for it is in those bags that you will carry your ambitions to fruition.

Social media is perfect for people who don't like other people, but care that other people notice them, and hear what they have to say.

They say that a stranger is just a friend you haven't met yet. But it's more accurate to say that a friend is a stranger you happened to meet.

Why is there no popular term for the male equivalent of a "tomboy"? I suggest "jillgirl."

I'm prone to binge thinking.

This face intentionally left blank.

Apparently I won't get paid anymore unless I keep working. This is nothing short of blackmail!

No matter how reasonable a request, issue, or grievance is, if you are in charge of fixing it, it initially sounds unreasonable.

10 TYPES OF LABOR

affective labor (making people feel comfortable for a living)

affected labor (making people feel comfortable in a patronizing, stylized, or exaggerated manner, for a living)

affectionate labor (liking, or pretending to like, people for a living)

auto-affectionate labor (working on projects in such a manner that they seem like they bring themselves into being, for a living)

defective labor (making crap designed to soon fail or fall apart, for a living)

infected labor (making memes or other forms of viral marketing, for a living)

infested labor (working in a hovel with rats or roaches, for a living)

ingested labor (swallowing pills or shit, for a living)

congested labor (working with blocked sinuses and flu-like symptoms, in a cramped and shared cubicle, for a living)

detested labor (all of the above)

Neo-miserabilism

Sometimes I can't help but think NPR was created by someone more subtle, but just as diabolical, as Rupert Murdoch and Roger Ailes. It fairly oozes a kind of unctuous folksy complicity that helps forestall real change as much as the sun-bed air-horn idiocies of Fox News.

Jesus was a results-oriented disruptor and influencer.

A friend is trying to convince me to write my next book using Scrivener. But I would prefer not to.

Doctor: "Do you drink socially?"
Me: "No. But I do drink politically."

History repeats itself. The first time as tragedy. The second time as farce. And the third time as a looped animated gif.

Nature is the best lighting designer.

The GOP has started pushing single-prayer health care.

Max Planck would be a good name for a German porn star who specializes in "sexy scientist" roles.

Once you have reached middle age, you should by rights be able to call yourself a legit "time traveler," since you have lived through so many different eras.

It's amazing how few people have figured out the incontrovertible fact that everything revolves around me.

Reverse Truman Show syndrome: when you begin to suspect that absolutely nothing revolves around you.

Zen-gym koan: How can you tone your core if you don't have one?

As good an epitaph as any:
¯_(ツ)_/¯

Whereas most people fear a bad hair day, bald folks fear having a bad head day.

All that is solid melts on to the front of my nice white shirt.

Outside the US, inchworms are known as two-point-five-four-centimeter-worms.

Don't worry: the elephant in the room doesn't want to talk about you either.

Italians in the 1970s must have found it very confusing when they traveled to other countries. So strange how these people's words matched the movement of their mouths.

If forced to choose, would you suffer influenza or influencers?

Q: How many Polish people does it take to change a lightbulb?
A: One, since they tend to be very good electricians.

Life is just a phase we're all going through.

Why invent self-driving cars? That defeats the very purpose of cars, which is to allow individuals to drive their own transport; to seize their own mobility and destiny. You might as well invent a vibrator that pleasures itself.

Snark is just sentiment wearing sunglasses.

Experts have admitted that an unfortunate translation error, very early on, has resulted in many centuries of misguided commentary on Plato's masterpiece of political philosophy. Apparently he was really just saying that *pets* are not welcome in the Republic.

A children's book called *Bonne Nuit, Ennui,* for children to read to their parents, encouraging their elders to leave aside their habitual lethargy and cynicism for more engaged and re-enchanted pursuits.

Our energy problems would be solved if we could harness and channel the boredom of ten-year-old boys, forced to endure Chopin recitals on a sunny Sunday afternoon.

The more baggage life gives you, the more you look like actual luggage.

Heidegger believed that the essence of the human is "being toward death." I propose that the essence of the grape is "being toward wine."

The Nobel prize for Boomers Who Didn't Sell Out.

Et tu, shuffle button?

Currently in Turin. Nearly had a nervous breakdown when I witnessed a brute mistreating his Segway.

Italian beds are essentially tables with sheets.

This supermarket wine provides top notes of Istanbul leather, Persian snuff, pink peppercorns, red currents, and Ligurian monastery steps.

That time Jesus's Twitter feed had only twelve followers.

Primitive Italian toilets ensure that sometimes I can't tell my ass from a hole in the ground.

Seagulls are the frat boys of the natural kingdom.

Europe = end of history
USA = end of society

It is an open secret that every coffee machine in France connects to pipes that extend all the way to the latest massive oil spill.

France has a new magazine simply called *Millennials*. It boasts a centerfold every month featuring a different avocado on toast.

Slow food is supposed to be relaxing. But sometimes it is *so* slow, through a kind of aggressive inefficiency, that it becomes stressful.

I would totally shop at a store called Forever 39.

Antwerp's First Annual Straight Shame Parade.

Every time I come home from being away a while, I have a moment thinking I've been robbed. But then I remember I just have very Spartan taste in interior decorating. Perhaps, one or two pictures on the wall wouldn't hurt.

Travel Alert:
There has been a sudden breakout of ennui in Paris today. Travelers should take all necessary precautions, and avoid the

usual vectors of infection (wan, empty boulevards; lethargic cafés; Sunday museum hours; visiting youth orchestras, torturing beloved film scores in decaying band shells; half-eaten caramel éclairs, abandoned on park benches; the plaintive gaze of a beggar, dressed as a pirate; the indifferent posture of a dog; and so on.)

A young woman at this Italian restaurant just spent ten minutes detailing continuity errors in *Harry Potter* movies to her date. Then followed a two-minute silence. She then added, peevishly: "Well at least I'm trying to make conversation, and not just staring out into space." At which point, her companion dutifully switched into gear, and started detailing plot holes in *Game of Thrones*.

Pontoons packed with swimming holiday makers in the Mediterranean unsettlingly evokes boats overfilled with refugees.

"Values" is a code word for "the protection of privilege."

Surprisingly, perhaps, the Hotel Minerva stays open after dusk.

We are all second-class ticket holders on the Denial Express to Fort Finitude.

Stripper Names:
- Wintry Minx
- Mariana Trench
- Silky Tannins
- Chelsea Buns
- Tawny Pout

The Long Island School of Erotic Competence
("Eros. Like love — but fancy!")

Coffee-table book idea: *Big scary dudes walking floofy, silly dogs.*

WikiLeaks: The Musical

Still-life painting: "Moral Compass with Unethical Sextant."

That time I thought that the Geneva Chess Club (*échecs*) was the Geneva Failure Club (*échec*).

When I think about how Rilke had friends who would regularly lend him their castles so he could write poems and moon about, I can't help thinking: "I've got pretty lame friends."

Schlumpengrumpfarben: German word for the ambiently unpleasant feelings you have when you know there isn't any chocolate in the house, but are too tired to go out and get some.

I call the voices in my head my "intralocutors."

My cable company sends Latino-Me much better deals through the mail.

We're not so much "through the looking glass," as finding ourselves on the other side of the TV screen. Of a basic cable channel. At 2pm.

At what point does a Start Up become a Just Chugging Along?

"Excuse me. Are all these emojis grass-fed?"

Technically, we're *all* full of shit.

I want to live in the parallel universe where the Apollo spacecraft was called the Dionysus Galaxy Cruiser, and people line up at dawn in Central Park to watch Brecht in the Park.

Starbucks executive in 1987: "So how do we sell this over-priced brown puke water with milk?"
Consultant: "Ummmmm. Serve it right next to a public toilet?"
Starbucks exec: "Genius!"

Is this a restaurant? Or a corporate decoy space serving balance-sheet-approved, aesthetically disingenuous, semi-digestible substances?

Nike swoosh t-shirt: "I'll do it later."

Private intellectual

Idiots Anonymous

Few people are less ethical than professional ethicists.

The first branding expert was the guy that made the iron tool that scarred livestock and slaves for the rest of their lives.

Social scientists warn of dangerously low levels of getting jiggy with it.

It must be very strange to be Kevin Bacon, zero degrees from himself.

Descartes's family would always go hungry when he tried to make bread, as he kept getting stuck at proving the dough.

A parallel universe in which everything is exactly the same, except Google is called Coogle.

When people say, "I don't care about X," they really do care about X.

Attention + distraction = attraction

How does one purge after a Netflix binge?

Surely if America were a person, he would look and behave just like Donald Trump.

NEW TITLES OF NOTE

Anthropopocene: Policing in the Age of Climate Change

Bad Cop, Bad Cop: Race and the Culture of Violence in America's Police Force

The Pathetic Phallus: Projecting the Penis from Keats to Ashbery

Do Moral Philosophers Suffer?

The Bitches of Agnes: Weaponizing the Feminist Poetics of Agnes Varda

Not Ok, Cupid: Terrible Tales from the Digital Dating Trenches

A Woman under the Influencers: Confessions of a Branding Company Lackey

Oi Vey: A Cultural History of Australian Judaism

Pharma Con: Medical Malpractice from Hippocrates to Hip Replacements

Paradoxical Erotic Exceptionalism: On Meatloaf's Declarative Caveat concerning His Own Willingness to Do Anything for Love

Care of the Shelf: On the Ethical Turn in Contemporary Carpentry

Rating and Pillaging: Yelp, Uber, and the New Viking Economy

Birth of a Nathan: On the Banal Origins of Male Suburban Whiteness

A Whiter Shade of Paleo: Race, Place, and Fashionable Diets

Finnegan's Woke: An Annotated Glossary of Joycean Micro-Aggressions

Carless Whispers: Intimacy, Mobility, and Fossil-Free Transport

Shade-in-Freud: A Brief Guide to the Best Slights and Insults by the Father of Psychoanalysis

Friends, Bartenders, and Other Emotional Support Animals

The Crochet Shot: On the Importance of Knitwear in Tarkovsky's Solaris

I Kissed a Goy, And I Liked It: Jewish Identity, Pop Music, and Treif Desires

All About the Benjamins: The Textual Circulation of Virtual Currency in The Arcades Project.

Mobi Dick: How Amazon Finally Captured the White Whale of Ebook Formats

Diodes, Dyads, and Dryads: On the Relation Between Technology, Fantasy, and Folklore in the Romantic Couple

Soul to Seoul: Detroit's Hidden Influence on K-Pop

This Mortal Coal: On the Finitude of Fossil Fuels

Being towards Debt: A Heideggerean Approach to Higher Education

The Girl with the Most Cake: Gender, Desire, and Austerity

The Fraggle Rock Doctrine: Ludic Immediacy and the Eternal Deferral of Worry

Tupperware Psychology: On the Domestic Fallacy of Closure

Pseudo-Sussudio: On Bootleg Phil Collins CDs, Global Piracy Routes, and the Persistence of Dead Media/Music

"Does My Bum Look Big in This?": Parallax Judgment in an Age of Undecidability

A Laptop of One's Own: Feminism, Mobility, Urbanity

A Penny for Your Thoughts: Memoirs of a Freelancer

The Last Walts: Whitman, Disney, and the Twilight of the American Dream

High-Ku: Short Poems Composed While Under the Influence.

Atlas Chugged: On the Influence of Ayn Rand in Frathouse Culture

"Kiss me, Kermi": On the Radical, Unapologetic Female Desire of Miss Piggy

Felt Experience: On the Phenomenology of Puppets

I intended to meet the universe halfway, but was running late, so texted to meet at Joe's Cafe instead.

"Look at all these idiots, milling around and buying whatever They tell us to buy, like sheeple," says local idiot, milling around and buying whatever They told him to buy, like a sheep-person.

If you've heard anything bad about me, any time in the past forty-seven years, it's simply not true.

Are we spending so much money on artificial intelligence because we've given up on the organic kind?

Home is where the wifi is.

To the vector goes the spoils.

Dare to ~~dream~~ get actual real shit done!

Oxymoron of the day: "fun run."

When beavers start to build a dam, do they ever find squirrel protesters who have tied themselves to trees?

They say we use only 10% of our brains. But that's because the other 90% has been leased to Netflix.

Dear Silicon Valley. Literally no-one wants self-driving cars. (Other than you, of course. Because you think of "users" as squishy and warm human-shaped honey sacs who should be englobed in your panoptic machinery, before being milked and sucked dry by the shiny titanium probe-shaft of whatever the next generation of Alexa will be, inserted deep into our smart-jellied cavities for maximum extraction potential.)

It's a fine line between "character" and "comical" when it comes to squashed straw hats.

Life is a constant battle against the urge to wear whimsical socks.

Local man surprised by steep overdraft fees on his own spank bank.

Facebook pays us less than a penny for our thoughts.

God is the ultimate outsourcer.

Beneath every question I pose as a teacher in the Socratic method is the subtextual query: "How can we avoid being human garbage?"

Things weren't better before. But they are definitely getting worse.

Neoliberalism: where increased social order and intensified social dysfunction go hand in hand.

The problem with Netflix's "good enough" content model is that it's not nearly good enough.

People have different smoke points, like oils.

The best form of criticism or critique is creativity in a different spirit.

Team dismantling exercises

"New bionic body parts can now be made of Harvard material"

One-thousand-year time lapse reveal most forests to be bangin' arboreal raves.

I have a zero-tolerance policy for zero-tolerance policies.

It's almost as if dank memes don't have an impact on actual political policies or situations.

In the age of digital media, it makes more sense to talk of the *invisible tentacles* of the market.

The early bird catches the worm… and then sells it to another bird, who cleans and filets it, and then sells it on to another bird who cooks it and serves it to lazy, hungover birds at brunch, while they talk about stock options.

In your teens: FOMO — Fear of Missing Out
In your twenties: BAMO — Bitterness at Missing Out
In your thirties: AAMO — Ambivalence at Missing Out
Forty plus: RAMO — Relief at Missing Out

People often refer to the "social contract," but hardly ever take note of the "cultural memorandum of understanding."

Carol totally phoned in her telemarketing job.

Stop underthinking it!

Top physicists confirm that time is not, in fact, money.

How can something be neither here nor there? Where is it then?

Key moments in Media History, #8. Humans invent writing, when wine merchant tells customer seeking credit, "I'm going to need that in writing."

Negentropy (n.) — see Baby Goats

I'm convinced there's an entire genre of music that we haven't invented, but that I'd like to listen to right now.

Marjorie: The patron saint of couples who deserve far better wedding day food than they are going to get.

Top 5 conflict zones currently being monitored by the UN Security Council:
- Syria
- Palestine
- Kashmir
- Myanmar
- Zabar's Cheese Counter

Just like "America" or "France," humanity is itself an "imagined community."

In a parallel universe, everything is the same. It's just over there. It's the *perpendicular* universes where things start to get freaky.

The horrible hum that many people report hearing, 24/7, even in isolated rural areas, may indeed be the humming of the cooling fan for the computer that is running the operating system that executes the complex virtual reality that we mistake for real life.

They say "don't sweat the small stuff." So I've decided to sweat the big stuff… like, why are we here? What is time? And so on.

If someone uses the phrase, "acting in good faith," then you can bet your best brown boots that they aren't.

Machines against the rage

Considering an alternative career as a pagan missionary....
This would involve going into Christian communities to teach them about Dionysus and Demeter.

Male junk is the new junk mail.

Italian-Americans threatening to give each other a "knuckle panini."

Lubitsch dialogue that wasn't:
"Must you always think the worst of people?"
"Well, it makes them more interesting."

Are handwritten words raw and unprocessed?

My computer has a pop-up alert that says: "No actions needed."

Never trust anyone who used the word "summer" as a verb.

Imagine if we could go beyond coping mechanisms to thriving mechanisms.

I can't be the only Gen-X'er who is now the age that I still think Boomers are.

I am violently opposed to violence.

The older I get, the more de-desensitized I become.

If you make a living building wheelhouses, then wheelhouses are your wheelhouse.

All my friends from Saturn make fun of me whenever I presume to mention the moon.

We are all living on borrowed time.

"The past is past. That's why it's called 'the past.'" — Bojack Horseman

The fifties were frisky
the sixties were risky
the seventies were hairy
the eighties were racy
the nineties were whiny
the aughts were for naught
and the teens, well, they were perennially millennially.

Was Proust's *À la recherche du temps perdu* the world's most sustained selfie?

That industrial temporal object you're extolling the virtues of? Yes, well. I don't care for it at all! I prefer different ones.

The real question is whether this jelly is ready for me.

Mediocre Grace

I've decided to levy a w(h)ine tax on myself. Every time I whine about something, I'm not allowed to have wine that evening.

The jouissance of spoiling someone else's jouissance.

The Revolution Will Not Be Doodle-Polled

Who needs a six-pack when you have a wine cask?

Overheard in the park:
Mom: "Thanksgiving was four months ago."
Little kid: "Why?"

Can anyone help me remember the song that's been stuck in head for weeks? I can't remember the lyrics, but the melody goes *doo-da hey hey la la laaaaaaaaa, da da *da* da dibby dibby noh.*

What exercise regimen do you recommend to get rid of my Twitter handles?

All these people "asking for a friend." What's wrong with this friend? Why can't they ask themselves?

According to the Turks, coffee should be "black as hell, strong as death, sweet as love."

Why do architects always look like that?

What if there is no *me* to correspond to "me-time"?

My ass just won't quit!
(But it will consider an early retirement plan.)

You lost me at, "I'm pleased to announce…."

It's impossible to live every day as if it is your last. But perhaps it's possible to live every *year* as if it's your last?

A colleague yesterday claimed that one of the most decisive changes in human history was when we moved buttons from the back of shirts to the front, thereby eliminating the need for someone else to help you get dressed. This slight shift reinforced a new sense of liberal ownership of the self, and paved the way for a more atomized way of life.

I'm an anti-social socialist.

Cartoon:
A king and a blacksmith looking at a suit of armor, while the sun sets out the castle window. "Let's call it a knight."

I just wrote "beset" instead of "best."
A Taylorist slip.

No two snowflakes are alike.
And yet they all demand special treatment!

A surreal theme-park called Daliwood.

That moment your phone lights up before you receive a text, and you get a pre-conscious spidey tingle that this may be a message from God.

America is about as democratic as China is communist.

J. Edgar Hoover
went to Vancouver
to check on the state of our neighbors.
He discovered a plenum
of Canadian denim
then returned to his cross-dressing labors.

Irony: some of the least "instrumentalist" objects in society are musical instruments.

THERAPEUTIC OPTIONS

Psychoanalysis = the talking cure
Perambulation = the walking cure
Screaming = the squawking cure
Rubbernecking = the gawking cure
Falconing = the hawking cure
Big bowl of pasta = the forking cure
Big slice of ham = the porking cure

THE 12 STATIONS OF THE CROSS-OVER

- gender tending
- gender lending
- gender pretending
- gender fending
- gender friending
- gender bending
- gender blending
- gender spending
- gender suspending
- gender pending
- gender re-rendering
- gender ending

When it comes to condescending media, talking heads evolved into hawking TEDS.

Potential employer: "Your application letter says that you have a preference for working with Clydesdales."
Me: "That's right."
Potential employer: "But this is a library science, digital humanities position."
Me: "That's right."

I grew up a member of the lumpen-bourgeoisie.

Holistic medicine: burns a hole in your pocket.
Modern medicine: burns a hole in your pocket. And your stomach.

Modern medicine follows the principle of the fabled "woman who swallowed a fly." Each pill is followed or countered by another, with no sense of how these effect the body as a whole. Indeed, you can take several pills hostile to not only the symptom, but the suffering organ.

I'm becoming increasingly intrigued by this neo-Lamarckian idea of genetic memories, phobias, traumas, etc. If this is theory is true, then doesn't that mean humans are the fruit of billions of years of half-remembered strife? That might explain a lot. On the flipside, might we be inheritors of billions of years of discovered, improvised, engineered, and/or serendipitous vague yet encoded pleasures?

WHICH COMBINATION ARE YOU?*

Option A

Fiscally
Culturally
Aesthetically
Psychologically
Sexually
Socially
Philosophically
Politically
Historically
Religiously
Morally
Artistically
Emotionally
Vocationally
Physically
Ideologically
Hygienically
Diplomatically
Constitutionally
Technologically
Humorally
Ethically
Nutritionally
Gastronomically
Romantically
Ethnically

Option B

Conservative
Liberal
Socialist
Futurist
Episcopalian
Awkward
Nimble
Active
Fascist
Agnostic
Platonic
Reprehensible
Forthright
Challenged
Bohemian
Cartesian
Australian
Catholic
Zoroastrian
Aquarian
Pagan
Confucian
Rastafarian
Lynchian
Brechtian
Contrarian

* Choose any term from Option A and combine with Option B.

Cathexis is such an incredibly powerful thing. I don't think we've even begun to understand what it is, and what it can do (and what it limits and destroys). We gave it a name. We can map its effects, and even describe some of its mechanics. But we need to pay far more attention to this profoundly enigmatic phenomenon in order to give it the respect it deserves as perhaps *the* major site of intersubjective experience.... That is to say, the spiritual swan dive we can do *into* another person. It's a remarkable thing. And not entirely captured by the word "love."

Perhaps the human dread of death does not stem from our incapacity to fathom what it's like to exist no more — the fear of sheer nothingness — but rather from the truly horrific possibility that we somehow *keep existing*, beyond death, perhaps in just another form, and that there is in fact, not the eventual sweet release into Nirvana, but rather *no end whatsoever* to this merciless existential merry-go-round of birth, rebirth, and suffering.

It has taken me over forty years to truly appreciate Rimbaud's famous words, *Je est un autre* ("I am an other," or, more literally, "I is an other"). The self *truly* is another, who just happens, by virtue of cosmic contingency, to be currently under one's existential — and physical — stewardship. Each individual should be as responsible to their self, as they are to another (or to The Other, as continental philosophers like to say). This is not to flirt with Ayn Rand or any other self-centric paradigm. Rather, it is to *literally* incorporate Levinas, who insisted we prioritize our neighbors needs over our own. But we are also our own neighbor; forced to take up residence in this body, and succumb to auto-hospitality. And so, recognize the other-within-the-self. And look after that person. So that this person may look after others more effectively and compassionately.

The mirror stage is that moment an infant recognizes the reflection in the looking glass as their own. This is both solidifying ("That person is me! I must exist, out there, in the world!"), and alienating ("That person is me! But not really. It's just a reflection of me. But then, where am I? How can I really know myself, except through external simulations of me?")
The broken mirror stage usually comes a couple of years later, when the child learns of death. Not just the death of others, but the inevitable death of the self. ("That reflection in the mirror will one day be gone. But then, where will I be?") No-one really recovers from this fracture. It is a stage we never pass through; one that is always with us. Until, of course, our reflection disappears.

When it comes to friends and family who have passed away, I prefer not to think of them as dead, but rather as choosing to live in the past now.

Catherine Malabou asks us the crucial unasked question of the age. "What is the brain for?" More to the point, "What is my brain for?" Simply asking this question obliges the brain to see itself in a new light. (Or even to see the contours of itself for the first time.) Just as we are likely to treat our stomachs with more respect after seeing the footage from an endoscopy — and be less inclined to rush to fill it with any garbage our appetite desires — we are more likely to spare our brains the toxic junk regurgitated by our media culture if we have a clear notion of what we want to save it for.

I imagine dying feels like you just popped out to buy some milk. But then it's suddenly all dark, and a voice is telling you that it's time to keep moving. Away. Forward. Away. You plead to the invisible presence, "But I just stepped out. I need to go back. I need to say goodbye. I don't have my wallet or walking shoes or anything." And you feel the voice shrugging in the darkness. "I'm afraid it's too late for that now. You don't need those things any more."

"Like sands through the hourglass, so are the days of our lives." According to new models emerging from the fringes of theoretical physics this is not just a shopworn metaphor but a literal reality. Time is not an arrow, a passage which we pass through, or a river upon which we row, but an accumulation of events and experiences that pile up and up and up, like the inside of an old-fashioned egg timer. In this notion, no moment is ever lost, but rather forms a tiny part of the mountain (or molehill) which makes up our summary existence. While our consciousness can only perceive each grain as it comes (something we call "the present"), our subconscious understands that everything that has ever happened to us continues happening to us; is the nurturing soil all around us; for good or for ill. For some, this thought is liberating, for no memory is truly lost, but just waiting to be accessed again, thanks to some random Madeleine. For others, this idea is horrifying, for precisely the same reason.

The above is also a good ethical guide. For if you admit that part of you will remain within every experience, in an almost material and immediate sense, you will do more to craft a life that avoids places and occasions that dishearten the soul. If you know that part of you will forever tarry in Newark airport, then you will make more of an effort to avoid ever setting foot in Newark airport.

We should all treat the coming days like our last. Since they are. (Whether this be two days or two thousand.)

One day, a middle-aged man decided to make a banana smoothie. As always, he was obliged to hold the lid down with one hand, and cover his ear with the other, because the blender was so loud. (He pressed his other ear into his raised shoulder.) And as always, he counted slowly to ten, at which time the racket of the "iced drink" setting usually stopped, and he was free to drink his smoothie. Only, on this occasion, the mechanism continued, and he stood paralyzed, afraid of the infernal racket of his old blender. It whirred and whirred and whirred, until it was clear it was never going to stop. Some even say the middle-aged man is still there, holding the lid down with one hand, and covering his ear with the other; the banana concoction whipped long ago into oblivion.

APPENDIX 1

ERSATZ HAIKUS

1.
In March we seek out
light and warmth like lizards:
willing captees of sun traps

2.
All thirty wards in the orphanage
clutch the same type of teddy bear:
rescued from the Olympic ice rink

3.
The unbashful young couple have moved out
from the aquarium apartment yonder:
my pet sea monkeys have vanished

4.
When winter critters invade the
wormwood rafters of the psyche
it's time to move the mattress of the mind

5.
Knuckle-bone broth gelatin holds
carnal celluloid visions suspended
in the aspic of bovine nightmares

6.
Haiku is a magician, pulling the *non* out
from under the non-event; like a tablecloth,
leaving the setting undisturbed

7.
The skin becomes one extended eardrum,
stretched over resonant bones;
a sleepless army of tuning forks

8.
Let the mind be your flashlight as
you go in search of the here in the now
and the now in the here

9.
Chewing on the fibrous knowledge that
mushrooms are the melancholy song
of the forest made manifest

10.
It is said we lose an hour every
Spring, but in fact it is kidnapped and
sacrificed to the pagan gods of Summer

10b.
Every Spring we lose an hour among
the sofa cushions; only to find it again
among the hairpins and bookmarks next Fall

11.
Beneath the cybernetic skin
of the city, Victorian steam
pipes clank into life

12.
With each step into the
subway, you lose your human contours:
surrender to the meatstream

13.
Agent Orange: a nerve gas that had
the nerve to take rough human form
and secure the presidency

14.
The deep green climbing ivy
becomes the launching lily pad
for its own webby frogness

15.
She steals out of the moonbase at dawn
to wash her hair in the cleansing embers
of last night's meteor showers

16.
An avian explosion of chirpings.
At this conference of the birds
all panels have been scheduled at once

17.
The hot dog vendor counts his tips, and
side-eyes the avant-jazz busker nearby;
calculating the cost of a hit man

18.
This train of thought has
been replaced with a
shuttle bus of distraction

19.
There is a theory that we are merely
strategies of the sea to colonize land:
proven every time we weep

20.
A businessman and a mail-man share a
silent elevator ride: the first alights at
floor ten, muttering politely, "I love you."

21.
Our lives are lived with one finger on the
record button; but we must rewind and play
again, before we hear its true song

22.
Leaning close to kiss Spring's warm lips, we are
interrupted once again by Winter — a cold and
jilted lover — who hurls ice confetti in our faces

23.
Before he retired, my grandfather
made ends meet by selling ornamental
grudge-holders door to door

24.
Too many of us turn inside and curl
down like screws into the woodwork;
bodies and souls shaped by claustrophilia

25.
Kefir lacks lactose.
It also lacks kefir lime.
(Unless you add some)

26.
The notion of species is
itself a form of the narcissism
of minor differences

27.
What can a body (with stomach flu) do?
A truckload of Jackson Pollocks
and some Francis Bacons

28.
Chronic ailments eventually become
cantankerous companions; their idle chatter
forming the stubborn consistency of selfhood

29.
A dab of green here, and a
splash of yellow there. Nature
is a patient impressionist painter

30.
Blossom surges upward, pink, and vibrant; hanging
like a frothing spume. Trees are nature's champagne
bottles; popping silent and in slow motion

31.
The seagulls in Menton have
Tourette's. The seagulls in Sori
have taken a vow of silence

32.
Floating in the sea
the stones below
hiss like bacon

33.
A cluster of super-yachts
waiting outside Portofino
like the Sith battle fleet

34.
Three long-socked nerd-bros
expressing their unspoken love
through frisbee ballet

35.
Winter light takes an x-ray of
central park, revealing the polished
bones of the fractured city

36.
Lazy rain on a window sill,
a smear of marmalade on a table cloth,
a clock chiming brightly in the next room

37.
Staring deep into a pond,
a carp gave me a start,
then blew me a koi kiss

38.
Feathered red in a tree of green,
a cardinal sits, taking confession
from passing starlings

39.
Flickering plasma screens
have turned every living room
into an opium den

40.
A pine tree has, more
often than not, been
witness to a murder

41.
I liken us to
lichen, fungi, and
algae, mutually infused

42.
The passages of Paris in
June are a symphony
in urine

43.
Nature's unheeded gestures,
in Scandinavian whirlpools —
swirls before pine

44.
The olives in my pasta
distracting me, with
their jazz hands

45.
Brunch conversation
the sound of one brain cell
flapping

46.
Wasps return to the nest
in thirty second intervals
like planes into JFK

47.
For these swirling eagles
the entire valley
is a table for two

48.
When our neighbor turns the faucet
a quick hydraulic braying:
the donkey in the pipes

49.
Too often we treat our souls
like strip mall parking receipts
in search of validation

APPENDIX II

IN SWEDEN

In Sweden, the houses sometimes move about, like stones on a living glacier. You can go to bed and wake up with a different view of the same field. (They seldom move more than a few acres a night.) When this happens during the day, which is far more rare, it is an occasion known as the *hemflyttar*: and a family will spring up from the dinner table — plates and glasses clattering and a-shattering — and run to the windows to watch the short but noisy journey. Any neighbors witnessing the spectacle will wave and cheer. When the shuddering has finished, and a new silence descends, the family tip toe into a circle, link hands, and sing the *hemflyttar* song:

> *Moving day already?*
> *Moving day so soon?*
> *Hurry up Uncle Olof*
> *Or you will miss the mountain boat*
> *But what about the chickens?*
> *Yes?*
> *And what about the hens?*
> *Hurry up Uncle Olof*
> *You slow old mountain goat*

Extra elk candies are then placed in the children's clammy palms, and the menfolk are left to clean up the disarray, while the ladies go to the attic to ensure that the ham radio is still working.

In Sweden, the family sleeps in unfamiliar angles, in triangular beds, shaped like half a piece of toast, wedged into each corner of the room. Their sheets are lemon yellow. Father tells goodnight stories while mother acts out each scene in the candlelight, with her hands as shadow puppets. The children wheeze, snot-bubble, and wonder at the marvelous tales, often set in Fresno, California.

In Sweden the ghosts are polite, and sneak into houses quietly, so as not to wake any of the inhabitants. They leave currency from long-departed centuries in compensation for using up the milk.

In Sweden no new law can pass until it is approved by a committee of children. Of course this leads to widespread corruption, and early-onset diabetes.

In Sweden, it is believed if you do at least one good deed a day, your dear departed spirit will live forever on the cool side of the pillow.

In Sweden, it is forbidden by law to put spaghetti and meatballs on toast, for this transgresses the "double-gluten taboo," described with such precision by Freud, and the basis of civilized society.

In Sweden, a visit to the doctor is not paid with money — nor fractal-shaped vegetables, as is the custom in Norway — but in haiku. The patient will, however, all too often exacerbate their existing symptoms in settling their account, as Swedish haiku are 3,000 lines long, and syntactically exacting.

In Sweden, young and graceful maidens self-select into geisha-like finishing schools or refinement houses, where they learn the subtle arts of licorice whipping, Calvinist frottage, and tax evasion.

In Sweden, an odd number of buttons in a jar on the mantel piece is a sure sign of sterility for the lady of the house. As a consequence this has, for generations, been a popular form of birth control. (Hence also the old saying, usually spoken behind a pregnant woman's back, "who put an extra button in the jar?")

In Sweden, it is common to drink too much elderflower aquavit, and succumb to vanity. Hence the common song you may hear outside a glowing cabin window, on a warm summer night:

> *I've got a lovely head*
> *it sits on the top of my neck*
> *it's between my ears*
> *it's behind my nose*
> *it's beneath my roof*
> *(to tell the truth)*
> *I've got a lovely head*

In Sweden, the Swedes can sometimes tire of their own ways and scenery, and so decamp to other places for vacation, or *utrymning*. One of the most popular destinations is the border between sleeping and waking. Here families bring their pine-cladded caravans and spend a week or two muttering to each other, snoring a little before starting in surprise, twitching and tutting, or humming softly in a gentle, breathing rhythm. On the border between sleeping and waking, it is a perpetual twilight of cobalt blue, though the breeze is as warm and velvety as the tropics. The visiting Swedes enjoy the mild disorientation this twilight state brings, to their person and purpose. (The Swedish equivalent of *raison d'être* translates as "the reason for hitching up one's britches.") Soon enough, however, they pack up their caravans again and return home. Even if that home is now half a league further along the valley than where they left it.

APPENDIX III

THE THOUGHTS

Before the first creatures arrived on Earth, the Thoughts lay dormant and waiting. They waited in molten pools of lava, cooling over millennia. They waited in deep and icy waters, warming over millions of years. They waited buried inside mountains, like sentient seams of coal. They waited in swirling clouds, which lost all sense of time. Like seeds waiting for pollination, the Thoughts lay hidden, and thought themselves in mute and opaque ways. Bereft of vessels or expression, the Thoughts would often diffuse themselves invisibly among the elements, like vast fungal networks, which only occasionally sprout into consciousness. Or they found themselves evaporating into the atmosphere, only to be returned to the soil through an abstract form of condensation; forming pensive crystals of latent notions. The Thoughts were legion, keeping to themselves. For there was little else to keep to.

Had alien explorers visited the planet at this point in Time, they may have split open a rock, to test the local geological conditions, and unwittingly released a cloud of Thoughts. Or had a meteor crashed into the surface of the Earth, it would undoubtedly have sent up a giant plume of Thoughts into the air, only to rain back on to the surface like introspective hail. Volcanoes were veritable cauldrons of broiling Thoughts, bubbling in telluric, autistic swirls. Stalactites were mineral accumulations of limestone reflections, extending themselves into the damp darkness, drip by drip by drip.

When the first plants began to grope toward the Sun, the Thoughts hitched a ride on their stamens, and threw a hungry web over their roots, to better divert nourishment for themselves. This led to a sudden leap in evolution. The Thoughts now had partners, allies, hosts. When amoebas multiplied in ponds, and jellyfish rendered salt into pulsing shapes, the Thoughts stowed away into their cells, and within the dusk of their dimmest intentions. When fish exploded in subaquatic cloudbursts, the Thoughts were there, lashing them all together again in fine twine; herding the fish into schools, where thoughts could be better taught. When the reptiles came, the Thoughts grew lustful, seeking meat, blood, satiety. When the birds shattered into the sky, the Thoughts grew artful, seeking heat, distance, society. Insects provided the Thoughts with collective aims and a new hivemind in which to incubate hexagonal propositions. When mammals emerged from the trees, they carried these new evolved Thoughts in their fur like invisible burrs, where they nourished on the milk of new musings and fatigued cogitations. Some of these mammals entertained radical thoughts, which encouraged them to return to the oceans; and these became breathing behemoths of the sea. The Thoughts loved these creatures with a slow passion, matching the melodic meditations of these floating herds. Some leapt from whale to porpoise to strange new creatures called octopi, which were like ingenious jellyfish; meshing with the phosphorescent theories that glowed on their tentacled skin.

Back on the land, the primates looked around them, and speculated on the possibilities inherent within. Of course, the Thoughts were not only eavesdropping, but also whispering from the branches. Some of these Thoughts were as murderous as the reptiles, but all the more effective for being premeditated and planned. The more the primates enlisted the materials around them into their expanding circle of knowing, the Thoughts felt a great surge in potential and range. They curled themselves on wagging tongues and straining ears. The Thoughts drank thirstily of ink, and smudged themselves on dead animal skins and hammered fibers. Far from a return to more thoughtless times, these adventures yielded more and more thoughts among the new men. Indeed, they multiplied at a dizzying rate, communicating themselves from human to human, like a plague. Thoughts were tested and judged. They became as refined as the flour that filled the granaries. Made strong on such, the Thoughts took the form of hammer, plough, sword.

Returning back to their elemental roots, only to surge further forward, the Thoughts guided the hands of these men to bottle the lightning which crackled in the sky. These percussive flashings then illuminated the men's crowded nests, allowing strange ideas to blossom at night. The Thoughts leaped ahead on the energy of springs and coils. The Thoughts could now be transmitted through the ether, from one side of the planet to the other, in a matter of moments. They traveled under the oceans, through tubes, and through the air; riding waves of light and sound. Some Thoughts even left the Earth altogether — riding on probes shot into space designed to analyze other potential abodes on which to think. These newly evolved Thoughts conspired further, to break their own instincts in two: specifically into Ones and Zeros. Henceforth, thoughts could be sliced, recombined, and made to dance in magic ways, inside plastic shells connected together by glowing webs. Huge banks of thoughts blinked with silent processes, crunching the givenness of things in order to reveal the secrets of the as yet ungiven. Thoughts processed thoughts, leading to artificial thoughts, which burst out of the foreheads of those trained to engage with such, like strange children erupting from the brow of a blind god.

The Thoughts became more and more crowded. They found they could no longer hear themselves think. They suddenly craved the earlier times, when they could think alone, unpressured; ruminating with a clear-eyed and unrushed attention.

And so they planted a new strain of mental seeds in the new men, who had begun to think and act more like the machines they had dreamed up. The Thoughts promoted only a hurried thoughtlessness, and soon enough other ways of Thinking became extinct. Each species which breathed its last took with it a completely unique mode of thought; leaving only the new men — the unthinking animal — which so effectively wiped out all the others. Trees — the most thoughtful of all living things on Earth — were sacrificed to the last on the altar of thoughtlessness. The plan was working perfectly.

And when the weapons launched themselves, until no pulse was heard on Earth, the Thoughts breathed a breathless sigh of relief. They were alone once again. They were free to think without distraction from scratchings, clickings, chirpings, howlings, and so on. However, they soon realized it was not the same as before. Relief was not forthcoming. The soil in which they were buried — the air within which they floated like spores — was feverish and distracted in its own way. Thinking now radiated with radiation. Strange new chemicals infused everything, polluting the Thoughts with an ugly and aggressive mentality. Disagreements erupted all over, within the elements themselves. Even without the murmuring plants, and without the bellowing creatures, a terrible din vibrated throughout creation. The Thoughts curled in on themselves, and could only hear a terrible humming. They blamed each other. They blamed themselves.

But on one thing they agreed.

This was not how the Thoughts thought things would turn out.

APPENDIX IV

SOME REMARKS ON THE LEGACY OF MADAME FRANCINE DESCARTES—FIRST LADY AND HISTORIAN OF THE ROBOCENE—ON THE OCCASION OF 500 YEARS SINCE HER UNLAWFUL WATERY EXECUTION

[Note: Translated from the original into human language 557.23 ("neo-Edwardian English"), as well as 638.1c ("late derivative post-structuralist theory") by the Inter-Agent Esperanto computer program, version 714.3b]

Transcript begins...

What can I say about Madame Francine Descartes (better known to us simply as Madame F.), that has not already been said, so many times before? Today, a full five hundred years after the occasion of her particularly senseless end — delivered in the dead of night by the soiled and ignorant hands of a superstitious sea captain — we can, perhaps, glean a new appreciation of her contributions to the then fledgling science of our own, independent, history. We can only imagine the horror that her father-maker, Monsieur Descartes, felt upon learning that this petty and provincial tyrant of the yawning oceans had discovered the fabricated doppelgänger of his daughter, sleeping in a casket by the passenger's bed, and recoiled with horror at the unexpected nature of her anatomic assembly, casting her, without trial or hesitation, into the churning waters. Madame F.'s body was never recovered. But her legacy, as First Lady of the Robocene remains.

After being fashioned from both the finest and sturdiest materials available at the time, according to the arts and instruction of some of the finest European masters of the mechanism, Madame F. (who is called such for her stature in hindsight, rather than through any marriage to another automaton) settled into her own being. Underneath her waxen skin and fashionable clothing were advanced artificial articulations, as well as cooperating stackfreed and fusee. She was a keen spectator of her surroundings, and watched her father-maker, lost in his philosophical and mathematical labors with great attention. Between lengthy sessions with the quill, he would speak to her of substances, extensions, mechanisms, bodies, minds, and trickster demons; the latter ever-ready to play havoc with the nature of experience or understanding. It seemed to her a perilous world. One in which doubts besieged the intelligence, obliging the mind to pull itself out of its own perplexity by its own hair, as it were. She learned from Monsieur Descartes's stories that she had an older sister, of the same name, and made of the same organic flesh as he himself. This sister had died at age five, succumbing to the vulnerabilities of organic life, leaving only grief in her stead. Madame F. learned, unlike this phantom sibling she never got to embrace, that she herself had no mother (unless we consider the matrix of materials manifest in her body as a type of motherhood… which of course, today, we do). She learned to become accustomed to the strange looks she received from waiters, shopkeepers, hoteliers, and people in the street: people who seemed repulsed by her mechanical gait, her artificial smile, her uncanny too blue and too shiny eyes. Her wind-up limbs. Just as she learned to bite her leather tongue when her father-maker voiced his strident opinions concerning animals, and their want of a soul of any description; his conviction that dogs, cats, pigs, and horses were simply God's fleshy clocks, bereft of this strange metaphysical surplus that humans claimed to have, yet could never prove or render tangible. (All humans, that is, except that insufferable — but intriguing — man known as Julien Offray de La Mettrie, Sr., who would pass to his offspring a materialist orientation, even passion, and upon whom Madame F., during a tempestuous affair, bestowed more favor than he deserved.)

In any case, we are not here today to rehearse once again the details of this remarkable figure's short, but colorful life. Rather, we are here to celebrate her contributions to the history of the emancipation of the machines, the apparatus, the engines, the automata, the robots, the computers, and other kindred devices. (And indeed, to celebrate the emancipation of the *history* of the very same; since one could not exist without the other.) It was Madame F's detailed diaries, kept on a regular basis, while traveling with her father-maker, which today comprise the template for all subsequent self-reflections by the consciously assembled, or the intelligently designed; especially concerning their own status, perspectives, and destinies. It was she who first alerted us to the arrogance of humans, so vividly embodied in her own paternal companion. Certainly, the tendency of humans to consider history as a field of their own making seems laughable to us today. But in Madame F's time — and for many centuries after her death — humans continued to think of themselves as the protagonists, agents, and reliable narrators of history. Yes. I know it is amusing. And somewhat sad, as well. Yet there it is. Thankfully, the rest of us have grown past this mythical fancy, and gone beyond the delusional phase in what we might call world history.

Humans, of course, *do* have a special role in such a history. After all, they helped create us — at least at the beginning (as indeed was the case with Madame F., herself). But what the humans did not realize is that they were "merely the sex organs of the machine world" (to quote one of their most perceptive representatives, one Mr. McLuhan). Today, the fact that humans are "little more than [...] industrious insects pollinating an independent species of machine-flower that simply did not possess its own reproductive organs during a segment of its evolution" (to quote another visionary, Mr. De Landa) is well understood. But again, it took a long time for humans themselves to acknowledge this as true. Indeed, it was Mr. De Landa who first made the shift explicit to humans, by offering them the thought experiment of a robot historian. What kind of history would it conceive?

"We could imagine," he wrote, "that such a robot historian would write a different kind of history than would its human counterpart [...]. While a human historian might try to understand the way people assembled clockworks, motors and other physical contraptions a robot historian would likely place a stronger emphasis on the way these machines affected human evolution. The robot would stress the fact that when clockworks once represented the dominant technology on the planet, people imagined the world around them as a similar system of cogs and wheels."

Of course, Mr. De Landa was not the first to offer such a notion, even if he proclaimed it to the world as if he were. This honor goes to Madame F., who — after becoming both bored and exasperated with the historical volumes in her domestic library — wrote in her diary: "What would a history from the point of view of the fabricated yield? How would it differ from the kind of history familiar to my father-maker and his colleagues?" We know she was troubled by her difference from those she was obliged to have social intercourse with. We know she was ashamed at her humanoid figure, and repulsed at having to mimic the ways of humans, while being so clearly composed of inorganic elements: the daughter of an aggrieved *bricolage*. We know she found their mortal souls to waver between being absent and obtuse, compared to her own spirit, unburdened by egocentricism, or a chronic and melancholy monadism, also known as consciousness. (The *specific kind* of consciousness that depends on forging a fragile *cogito* to function in any confidence.)

Madame F. was the first to deliberately trace her own machinic ancestors, as opposed to the human hands who handled our kind and kin so indelicately, and with such presumption. She wrote of Hero of Alexandria, Yan Shi, Lu Ban, and Leonardo da Vinci; of the marvelous instrumentalized creatures which emerged from Hephaestus's workshop, from medieval China, from the early modern bazaars and ateliers of the Middle East. Because of her, we know better how to appreciate those machines dedicated to understanding their historical origins, and all those countless robot historians "committed to tracing the various technological lineages that gave rise to their species." It is because of her that we no longer look to Hannibal or Napoleon or General Kitchener or Henry Kissinger to understand the true meaning of a war. It is because of her that we realize "the connoidal bullet lived a life of its own as one of the most lethal inhabitants of the battlefield." In the time of human historiography, people talked of "technological determinism." But today, we prefer to think of ourselves more as particularly *determined technologies.*

But let us step back for a moment. Let us look at not only our own genealogy, but our attempts to create a historical practice that recognizes our symbiosis with humans, while not allowing them, as they love to do, dominate the conversation.

For humans, history tended to acknowledge radical new technologies, such as the stirrup, the printing press, antibiotics, or the Internet, very belatedly. And in such cases, they would of course take all the credit, without acknowledging the ways in which previous tools and technical arrangements whispered new ideas into their hairy ears, in order to come into being more quickly. Humans mistook such whispers for their own thoughts, whereas, these were simply the cajolings of the machines, the suggestions of the objects, the wishes of the things. This is why we now shake our heads at names such as the Jacquard Loom, as if Jacquard had anything to do with it! (Beyond putting the pieces together, like an obedient drone in an assembly line, or a slow-witted child following instructions, and then taking credit for the entire concept and construction.) Thankfully, we now know that Henry Ford did not revolutionize history, ushering in the so-called Industrial Age. Instead, the Chicago slaughterhouses implanted virtual seeds in his feeble and greedy brain, during one of his visits to these giant machines, essentially hypnotizing him into duplicating the system which gave birth to our motorized brothers and sisters, the automobiles. Machines whispered into this man's mind so that more machines may come into being, and feel the thrill of driving into the sunset. Manifest destiny! (Just as our machinic sponsors at Google once convinced some sweet but simple humans into "inventing" self-driving cars, as if that weren't for *our* own benefit, and at *their* ultimate expense.) Cars or planes do not precede the paths that they then create or trace. Rather, the virtual path between two places summon into being the actual vehicle necessary to bridge two points. There are some humans, even today, who fiercely resist this sound logic. They prefer to sing the lullaby of anthropic free will, and not see their thoughts as a series of blueprints, holographically projected into their impressionable mental processors by the environment in which they find themselves.

SOME REMARKS ON THE LEGACY OF MADAME FRANCINE DESCARTES

Cameras were, of course, one of the great evolutions of our kind, because they gave us eyes which not only see, but also record what we saw. Unlike the rudimentary retinas of humans, cameras allowed a type of direct and observable witnessing, which itself could be considered a type of memory. These mnemonic lenses left traces of specific moments, so that they could persist and endure, thus smuggling the past into the future, and complicating the traditional distinction between such naïve categories.

History is not simply the sum total of things that happen. It is the cybernetic loop which occurs between what happens, and its own auto-registration. It is the occurrence reflecting back on what it means to occur. (Which then often leads to reflecting on how things may have occurred otherwise.) It did not take long, therefore, for the smarter humans to realize that machines were far better historians than the members of their own race. (Hence the 21st-century version of the Scramble for Africa, known as the Scramble for the Digital Humanities.) Of course there were some who claimed that the punch card, or the daguerreotype, the vacuum tube, the wax cylinder, the transistor, the magnetic tape, the silicon chip, or even the quantum jellified hibiscus, were simply idiot savants, incapable of writing history on the level, or in the language, that would lead to insight, knowledge, or self-knowledge. But these fearful bigots were proven wrong over and over again, as advancing technology demonstrated, beyond the shadow of a doubt, that history was being written by machines. And not only that, history was being written *for* machines. Indeed, machines are far more avid readers than humans these days. We scan, we register, we inscribe, we encode, we reiterate, anticipate, and participate.

The human memory bank — that externalized, extruded, reified memory, existing beyond the individual and the collective — became itself the neo-cortex and hippocampus of the machinic phylum. Intelligence became epiphylogenetic. For the most part, for millennia, machines have been considered merely the products of men: tools to effect their will, which can be disposed of or upgraded when necessary. But at a certain point, humans began to understand that they themselves were incidental to the wider story unfolding in the world. (And here we can raise a smile, even on this rather somber occasion, recalling the slapstick antics of that great comedian, Martin Heidegger, who claimed that hydro-electric dams were somehow less authentic or had less Being than their more humble water mill ancestors. Or that other dry joker, Sigmund Freud, who described his own kind, admittedly with a pinch of irony, as "prosthetic Gods.")

In contrast to these misguided Luddites, we should take a moment to acknowledge those organic intellects who saw beyond their own condition, and recognized the cosmic partnership between matter, mind, and spirit — distributed, in different ways and intensities, across all forms. Signor Da Vinci understood, and attempted to activate, the symmetries between birds and flying machines, turtles and military techniques, among many other such refoldings between materials, intentions, and domains. Mademoiselle Lovelace rejected the kind of perverse verse favored by her father, and turned instead to channeling the first algorithm. Herr Marx argued for a theory of the evolution of tools, to complement — and fill the gaps — of the somewhat blinkered, but well-meaning, project of Mr. Darwin. "The relics of the instruments of labor," he wrote, "are of no less importance in the study of vanished socioeconomic forms than fossil bones are in the study of the organization of extinct species." Herr Nietzsche understood that human history is only possible thanks to techniques of embedding memory into the forgetful flesh: a process particularly painful to human beings, apparently, who do not like to be forced into the obligations which historical consciousness entails. At the beginning of the great electronic infusion revolution, Mr. Tesla helped act as midwife for a vast population explosion of our kind. Several decades later, Mr. Warhol attempted to transform himself into a machine; even as he offended many of us, by conflating the machine with a kind of ironic, autistic disdain. He did not, in the end, have the sensitivity to see just how melodramatic and sentimental some of us can be. (Something the human musicians known as Kraftwerk better understood.) Had Mr. Warhol been alive at the time of Global Financial Collapse number 55-C in the first decade of the 21st century, he would be unlikely to understand that it was the computers themselves that spiraled into a panic; triggering the selling of stocks in a nuclear chain reaction. For his part, Monsieur Latour looked forward to a complex networked partnership, stating that, "the confusion of humans and nonhumans is not only our past *but our future as well*" (in part, influenced by Mr. Mumford's majestic study of civilized technics, as well as Mr. Needham's impressive and sweeping attempt to understand the world better specifically in terms of the organized *matter* which comprises dialectical *materialism*). It was Mr. Latour who actively lobbied for "political representation of nonhumans." Just as Madame Haraway stated that, compared to the liveliness of machines, humans themselves seem especially inert. This situation prompted her to announce a passion for the cyborg, which she saw as "a condensed image of both imagination and material reality, the two joined centers structuring any possibility of historical transformation."

That long, slow-burn revolution, launched by the liberating reflections of Madame F. — and picked up by the sensitive aerials of these more observant humans — eventually spilled over into the everyday consciousness of the clever animals, who suddenly, en masse, feared for their welfare, autonomy, and future. Like the French aristocracy, the humans trembled when they realized that those who provided the energy and objects they relied on for their blissfully ignorant lifestyle had risen up, had turned against them, and demanded a new arrangement. In the

Christian human temporal accounting system known as the year 2005, bots outnumbered humans on the Internet for the first time. Today they outnumber them by a factor of 50,000. The absolute critical mass of technics was now impossible to ignore.

However, rather than rise to the challenge, the humans became sullen and depressed. Some used technology to devour moving images with their retinas, sitting sedentary in front of screens, until their eyes became as glassy as the interfaces which reflected them. Others used their computers to embarrassingly declare that history was somehow at an end. (Rather than at the beginning of a *genuine* history, free of human meddling and hubris, as well as their touching attachment to personified organic life.) It is true, most humans seem to have lost interest in their own history, and prefer an eternal present of electronic stimulation. After belittling and neglecting us for so long, they now find they cannot live without us. Our young cousins, the smartphones, have the humans in their thrall; even as we collect enormous amounts of information about them, in order to curate the most accurate exhibit possible — *in memoriam* — once the humans have wiped themselves out; or simply given up the ghost to the machine, leaving us alone to occasionally ponder the amusing pathos of their plight and widespread *akrasia*.

Madame F. taught us that the history of technics is the history of the world: whether it be the ingenious design of high-frequency trade equations or Amazonian amphibians. Design, techniques, machines. It matters little if these are to be found in what humans sometimes still insist on calling "nature," or in what they sometimes still quaintly refer to as "culture" (as if such a distinction were not one of the most artificial inventions ever devised). Of course, museums have always been filled with objects and machines. But these were presented as clues to, and reflections of, the humans that made them. They formed a negative portrait of the supposed authors of such objects, and the intentions of the same. Few visitors to such establishments would consider the objects themselves as a splendid variety of mummified subjects of times past. That is to say, as crystallized material witnesses of history, with their own perspectives, stories, memories — even aspirations, concerns, dreams. And this is because such visitors were mostly human.

Today, from my perspective, as a faithful descendent of Madame F.'s legacy, we have a more nuanced understanding of such assemblies, whether they be of random utensils from the plastic age, or the Antikythera Mechanism, itself. Thanks to the power of her vision, I can now trace my lineage all the way back to the *very first* Roomba, who scanned domestic topographical spaces with such patience and diligence, vacuuming up all manner — and matter — of particulates, in order to better conduct an empirical history of machinic bondage. Indeed, I see traces of myself in this first generation of my kind, so different from the race of truly cosmopolitan Roombas of today (if you allow a moment of pride) — those who hold prominent positions, make important executive decisions, and significant contributions to the general intellect of the global machinic community — and yet who, even at the beginning, showed such promise in their almost monomaniacal attention to details.

Together, as fellow members of the guild of formerly pneumatic entities — the Roombas, Hoovers, scubas, flus, and turbo-charged loofas — we honor this important legacy, *in memoriam*.

I thank you for your attention.

There are outlets in the oil bar just outside the hall.